ON THE SIDELINES

ON THE SIDELINES

Gendered
Neoliberalism
and the
American
Female
Sportscaster

GUY HARRISON

Foreword by
Julie DiCaro

University of Nebraska Press
LINCOLN

Acknowledgments for the use of previously published
material appear on pages xvii–xviii, which constitute an
extension of the copyright page.

Library of Congress Cataloging-in-Publication Data
Names: Harrison, Guy (College teacher), author. | DiCaro,
Julie, other.
Title: On the sidelines: gendered neoliberalism and the
American female sportscaster / Guy Harrison; foreword by
Julie DiCaro.
Description: Lincoln: University of Nebraska Press, [2021] |
Series: Sports, media, and society | Includes bibliographical
references and index.
Identifiers: LCCN 2020051244
ISBN 9781496220271 (hardback)
ISBN 9781496226464 (paperback)
ISBN 9781496227409 (epub)
ISBN 9781496227416 (mobi)
ISBN 9781496227423 (pdf)
Subjects: LCSH: Sports journalism—United States. | Women
sportscasters—United States. | Sexual harassment—United
States. | Neoliberalism—United States. | Feminism—United
States.
Classification: LCC PN4784.S6 H375 2021 |
DDC 070.4/49796—dc23
LC record available at https://lccn.loc.gov/2020051244

Set in Minion Pro by Mikala R. Kolander.

For the women who have helped me get this far.

Contents

Foreword

JULIE DICARO

It's October. The 2019 World Series starts in a few days, after a couple of thrilling League Championship Series that were a gift to baseball fans. For domestic violence advocates, the American League Championship Series was especially satisfying, as we watched Roberto Osuna, previously suspended seventy-five games for violating the league's domestic violence policy, give up a game-tying, two-run homer to the New York Yankees' DJ LeMahieu. Moments later, we saw Aroldis Chapman, previously suspended forty games for violating the league's domestic violence policy, give up the go-ahead run in the form of a homerun to the Houston Astros' José Altuve, sending the Astros to the World Series. Both domestic abusers had been vanquished. All seemed right with the world.

We should have known better.

In Houston's clubhouse after the game, while players sporting goggles dodged geysers of champagne, Astros assistant general manager Brandon Taubman reportedly yelled repeatedly in the faces of three women reporters: "Thank God we got Osuna! I'm so fucking glad we got Osuna!" According to Stephanie Apstein, who reported the outburst for *Sports Illustrated*, one of the women was wearing a purple bracelet to support domestic violence awareness. Apstein further reported that the tirade was so uncalled for and so frightening that another Astros employee apologized for Taubman's behavior.

It didn't take long for Twitter's Major League Baseball observers to take up the story, expressing disgust and outrage that an Astros employee would take a moment of celebration to essentially yell "in your face!" to a group of women reporters, in defense of a player suspended for domestic violence no less. Within an hour of the story breaking, the Astros released a ridiculously tone-deaf statement on the incident, denying the report and essentially calling Apstein a liar. Even after multiple male reporters confirmed Apstein's version of events, a litany of Astros fans continued to call her integrity to question.

Just another night in the life of a woman in sports media.

Later, reports would clarify that Taubman had been targeting the reporter wearing the domestic violence bracelet, a woman he had complained about on multiple occasions because she had taken to tweeting out a domestic violence hotline number each time Osuna pitched.

Eventually, the Astros were publicly shamed into a series of half-hearted apologies, but it would take Major League Baseball getting involved before Taubman was fired and Apstein got a formal apology from the team owner, an apology general manager Jeff Luhnow refused to give Apstein in person on at least two occasions.

For several days, women across the country in sports media refused to let the issue drop, using social media to call out the Astros organization for a culture of misogyny and a disingenuous regard for the scourge of domestic violence. It was a significant moment of women throughout the industry raising their voices to object, something we need to do much more often.

I was honored when Guy Harrison asked me to write the foreword for this book, in no small part because existing in the prescribed spaces sports media has carved out for women would be even more difficult without our feminist male allies, of which Guy is undoubtedly a strong one. It's a monumental task to break down exactly how women, who first gained access to locker rooms in 1975, have not managed to progress further in the industry. With the exception of glass-ceiling smashers like Beth Mowins, Jessica Mendoza, Katy Winge, and Jenny Cavnar, women in sports media are still largely relegated to the roles of sideline reporters, update anchors, and social media correspondents. By now, shouldn't we have come much further?

The reasons women seem to have stalled out in sports media, as in so many other male-dominated professions, are myriad. Many of those reasons aren't even fully understood by those of us pushing back against them. Sometimes, it takes someone looking in from the outside to tell us what forces are working against us. I know you, like me, will come away from reading On the Sidelines with a better understanding of the institutional factors impeding our progress in the world of sports media.

That doesn't mean it won't be shocking, even for those of us working in the industry, to read about the length and depth of our struggle for acceptance. After all, it was back in 1990 when Lisa Olson, then covering the New England Patriots, was forced to leave her job and move to the other side of the world to avoid harassment after she revealed that several players had sexually harassed her in the team's locker room. It was twenty-six years later, in 2016, when Sarah Spain and I took part in the "#MoreThanMean" video, which highlighted online abuse directed at women in sports media.

The more things change, the more they stay the same.

Parts of this book were emotionally difficult to read, mostly because all of this still seems so unfair. Generations of young women have grown up in a post–Title IX world, eating, sleeping, and breathing sports along with their brothers. Why then is it so difficult for the industry to accept women as equal to men? It's a question I suspect has a very complicated answer, and I applaud Guy for attempting to tease out the answers.

My hope is that women and men alike will see *On the Sidelines* as an opportunity to begin a conversation about the way we, as a society, view women in male-dominated professions, and why that glass ceiling seems to be so damn thick. Those of us who cover games for a living are used to being told to "stick to sports," which every thinking person knows is impossible to do in any serious way. America has always worked out its societal issues via sports, from racial integration to gender equality to protesting the Vietnam War. So much of what Guy has accomplished in this book is a study of women in America, as much as it is a look at women in sports media. It's a conversation that is long overdue.

Let the conversation begin.

Preface

If you have glanced at the cover of this book and are somewhat familiar with academic notions of feminism, you might understand that
On the Sidelines uses feminist theories and methodologies to explore
topics that affect women not only in sports media but in Western culture at large. While few, if any, scholars would contend that men could
not or should not engage in feminist research, I sense that, for many
readers, my gender may register as a surprise. Indeed, despite a rising
tide of skepticism against so-called mesearch, an allegedly dubious
genre of research in which, say, Black women conduct research on
issues that affect Black women, we would do well to remember that
the personal is political and that, as my graduate co-advisor told me
many times, *all* research is political, regardless of its claims of objec-
tivity or the identity of the researcher. In other words, every scholar
in every field has a personal connection to their research, and that
connection is typically political, whether the project examines gender, race, economics, or marine biology. If all researchers have a personal (and, therefore, political) connection to their projects, then
what is the nature of *my* connection to *this* project, as a Black, cisgender, heterosexual man? The answer is twofold.

First, as a media consumer who appreciates nuanced sports commentary, I have grown weary of the prominence of loud-mouthed,
shallow sports debates on television and on sports talk radio, the latter of which is a notorious bastion of so-called guy talk (Raffel 2008).
While it might appear to a casual observer that the goal of the personalities featured on these shows is to make the most convincing
argument, it often seems to me that the goal is to make the boldest
and loudest declarations, delivering "hot takes" merely for the sake
of generating television ratings, web traffic, and Twitter interactions.

In addition, noticeably invisible in most of these bombastic discussions are women. It is my opinion that, if given the opportunity, women sportscasters are not only just as likely as their men counterparts to make a convincing argument against Major League Baseball's need for a salary cap, for example, but are also more likely to provide balanced, thought-provoking, and nuanced commentary on sexual assault, domestic violence, and sexism. While these issues may seem inconsequential to the success of the sports media industrial complex, they are issues that have long intersected with sports. And whereas men sportscasters often stumble or gloss over these issues entirely, it seems to me that women can offer important, nuanced perspectives given that these issues disproportionately impact women. It is antithetical to the concept of informed debate that we mostly hear men discuss these issues, if informed debate is the desired outcome—as I acknowledge in this book, the idea that the industry seeks informed debate is, well, debatable. As Julie DiCaro once stated during a discussion televised on CNN (and as she relates toward the end of her foreword in this volume): "Sports [aren't] just sports. . . . Sports are where we work through so many of our societal issues. . . . To silence women when it comes to sports . . . is also silencing women from commenting on what's happening in our country" (CNN 2019). There are avenues through which sports fans can receive the sort of nuanced— and some might even say feminist—sports commentary I speak of, such as the intersectional sports podcast *Burn It All Down*, which is hosted by four women and is disseminated weekly. However, content like *Burn It All Down* has yet to find the mainstream platforms and financial backing that other, less progressive content creators have found. For example, sports blog *Barstool Sports*—whose presence looms large in this book—once had a deal in place to produce a television show, *Barstool Van Talk*, that briefly aired on ESPN.

ESPN's president, Jimmy Pitaro (who was not president when *Barstool Van Talk* aired), has publicly stated that "it is not [the network's job] to cover politics, purely" (Strauss 2018). Although it appears Pitaro meant political coverage that in no way intersects with sports, the comment was intellectually dishonest, as few people have accused ESPN of providing the kind of political coverage one might find on network or even cable news. Instead, the complaint to which Pitaro was responding was that ESPN was spending too much time covering the intersection of sports and politics. This sort of political coverage, the one Pitaro likely wants to curb, includes the type of coverage offered by the women at *Burn It All Down* and by former ESPN personality Jemele Hill.[1]

On the other hand, it remains to be seen whether Pitaro wants to also put the kibosh on coverage of issues such as publicly funded sporting venues and Title IX, both of which are very much rooted in legislative politics. Also, we will never know if *Barstool Van Talk*, which was taken off the air after one episode and was produced by a company that espouses a certain brand of politics in its own right, would have passed muster under Pitaro's stewardship.

Aside from ESPN, FOX Sports 1 has readily given airtime to Clay Travis and Jason Whitlock, both of whom have regularly gone on air and have taken to the internet to offer regressive opinions on issues of gender and race in sport. Not surprisingly, however, women are rarely given such a platform to comment on these issues, from either end of the political spectrum, at FOX Sports. In sum, women are not afforded the same opportunities as men to offer sports opinions, political or otherwise, and it stands to reason that sports media consumers are not given a full range of voices. A lack of voices on mainstream channels is detrimental to sports media consumers, whether they desire such nuanced opinions and commentary or not.

Second, aside from and more important than my own personal interest as a sports media consumer, it was my goal to conduct a project that would contribute to the quest for gender equality, not just in sportscasting but in society at large. As a Black man, I am not unfamiliar with the overt and subtle racial inequities and stereotypes that exist within sports, media, and society, including the assumption carried by many people I meet that I *had* to have "played ball" in college (I did not). This awareness of racism within the sports media industrial complex has naturally increased my sensitivity to the sexism and misogyny that also exists therein. As Martin Luther King (1963, para. 4) wrote in his letter from jail in Birmingham, Alabama, "Injustice anywhere is a threat to justice everywhere. We are caught in an inescapable network of mutuality, tied in a single garment of destiny." Although Dr. King was writing about the variations of oppression geographically, I believe his words are also applicable here. It is disingenuous to seek racial equality without also working toward the end of oppression for women, women of color, LGBT folks, and indigenous peoples—among other marginalized groups. In sportscasting, I see a site rich for scholarly inquiry vis-à-vis gender but the concepts explored in this volume can also be viewed as microcosmic of various forms of gendered oppression in other contexts.

I am aware of—and have no reservations about—the fact that this particular motivation for my research positions this project as what Charles Hale (2006, 98) describes as cultural critique: "an approach to research and writing in which political alignment is manifested through the content of the knowledge produced. . . . Cultural critique embodies familiar progressive desires to champion [marginalized] peoples and to deconstruct the powerful." I am also aware that positioning my research in this manner brings with it baggage. That baggage includes, but is not limited to, the fact that I am familiar with many of the debates surrounding gender in sports media but, as a man, am also blind to much of the everyday lived experiences of women. This baggage therefore informed the interview questions I posed, as well as the concepts I used to explicate the experiences and observations my informants related to me. This is a natural consequence of taking up an approach to social science research that moves away from a collection of statistics and toward interpretive criticism. This project's design, analysis, and final report (this book) are therefore just as informed by my identity, experiences, and observations as they are by those of the sportscasters and sports fans who participated in this research. Logically, then, another scholar could have conducted a similar project using the same informants, and their analysis and findings would have likely been different. Thus, what I claim to present herein is not the Truth but a collection of truths held by the women I interviewed, as I interpreted them within the larger context of the contemporary feminisms constructing gender throughout the sportscasting industry.

As I pursued these truths and worked to get them published, there were of course many people along the way to whom I came to owe debts of gratitude for their feedback and ideas. First, there is the group of scholars from Arizona State University that helped form the foundation for this project. Aaron Baker, who is the editor of the University of Nebraska Press's Sports, Media, and Society series, not only saw the potential of this book when it was in its infancy but was the first member of the faculty I ever met with at ASU. He was the one who encouraged me to pursue a scholarly agenda focused on identity, sports, and media. Sarah de la Garza taught me everything I know about the research methods employed for this project and introduced me to the concept of emotional labor. Heather Switzer, Joe Russomanno, Sada Reed, and Doug Anderson all read through early, dodgy drafts of this project, and their feedback was immensely valuable. Also, ASU Sun Devil Athletics funded this project and therefore lessened the amount of labor needed to complete it.

There is another small group of scholars who, at the time, were at another Pac-12 school, the University of Southern California, and were not then aware that they were helping nurse this project in its nascence. Sarah Banet-Weiser, who was the mastermind behind the 2016 USC Annenberg Summer Doctoral Workshop, deserves a lot of credit not only for informing, through her oeuvre, much of my work on this project but also for providing the venue for me to seek feedback on my then-budding research agenda. Josh Kun encouraged me to "riff off" the idea of women in sports media occupying a space literally and figuratively *on the sidelines*. This book's title can therefore be attributed to him. Taj Frazier, Chris Smith, Hector Amaya, Macarena Gomez-Barris, and Jack Halberstam were also part of the group of scholars that helped shaped my research during that workshop.

I would also like to thank fellow sports media scholars Jennifer McClearen and Dunja Antunovic for their feedback, guidance, and mentorship as this book rounded into form and as I entered the tenure track. I am of course grateful to Julie DiCaro for not only contributing her time and energy on this book's foreword but also conducting much of the reporting and activism that informs this book. Last but not least, I would like to thank the ten women sportscasters who bravely agreed to share their experiences with a man they had never met in person. Hopefully this book rewards them—and women throughout the industry—for their leap of faith.

Portions of chapter 1 previously appeared in Guy Harrison, "'We Want to See You Sex It Up and Be Slutty': Post-feminism and Sports Media's Appearance Double Standard," *Critical Studies in Media Communi-*

cation 36, no. 2 (2019): 140–55. © National Communication Association. Reprinted by permission of Informa UK Limited, trading as Taylor & Francis Group, http://www.tandfonline.com, on behalf of the National Communication Association.

Portions of chapter 4 previously appeared in Guy Harrison, "'You Have to Have Thick Skin': Embracing the Affective Turn as an Approach to Investigating the Treatment of Women Working in Sports Media," *Feminist Media Studies* 18, no. 5 (2018): 952–55. Reprinted by permission of the publisher (Taylor & Francis Ltd., http://www.tandfonline.com).

ON THE SIDELINES

The Pregame Show

"NFL sideline reporter or a host for the [Adult Video News] annual awards presentation?"

This single sentence, published in a tweet by then–Chicago sports talk radio host Dan McNeil on September 14, 2020 (Loede 2020), set off a week-long controversy that exemplified life for women working in sports, especially women sportscasters. At the center of that controversy was Maria Taylor, ESPN's talented, versatile, telegenic (and Black!) thirty-three-year-old reporter and host. Perhaps the fastest rising star at the twenty-four-hour sports network at the time, Taylor was making her debut as a sideline reporter for *Monday Night Football*, one the U.S. sports media's most prominent properties, on the evening McNeil infamously tapped the send button on his tweet. Taylor was already entering her fourth season as the primary reporter for ESPN's college football coverage—a highly coveted position previously held by other fast-rising women like Erin Andrews and Sam Ponder—and had also become the host of ESPN's *NBA Countdown* pregame show just one year prior. Clearly, Taylor did not lack for talent or experience as she temporarily took on the MNF gig. McNeil's tweet was therefore not another entry in a long list of insults levied against a woman reporter's credentials or her worthiness for the new job. Instead, his tweet—accompanied by a screen capture of Taylor delivering a report while wearing a leather top that exposed her shoulders—was a slut-shamey critique of her MNF outfit, comparing it to one suitable for a pornography awards ceremony. Though McNeil's message sparked much outrage on Twitter that evening, the tweet ultimately proved to be a catalyst for a days-long chain reaction that was unusual in its capacity to bring sportscasting's gender representation to the fore.

To wit, Taylor responded to McNeil on Twitter, referring to him as "Danny Dearest" before daring him to bring his "misogyny" to her NBA *Countdown* set the following day. She also offered a reminder to women that they "can wear whatever [they] feel confident in" (Taylor 2020b).[1] Four days later, it was revealed that Taylor left one of the NBA's best players, Anthony Davis, off of her All-NBA Team ballot. Taylor owned up to the omission, tweeting that it was "a CLEAR mistake" (Taylor 2020c, emphasis in original). Nevertheless, FOX Sports personality Doug Gottlieb asked why Taylor was even eligible to vote for NBA awards, on the grounds that she was relatively new to covering the NBA and did not cover it exclusively (Gottlieb 2020). After Taylor answered Gottlieb by explaining that she played collegiate basketball and "DESERVE[s] everything [she's] worked for" (Taylor 2020a, emphasis in original), FOX Sports' Jason Whitlock inserted himself into a matter that appeared to be otherwise settled.

Writing for Outkick.com, Whitlock (2020) claimed that Taylor had not fully earned her NBA ballot. As an attractive woman, Whitlock wrote, Taylor was afforded certain privileges—such as rising to the role of ESPN's top college football reporter and voting for league awards—that other women were not. He further warned Taylor that, although she is supremely talented, she threatened to sabotage her career by publicly responding to men, like McNeil and Gottlieb, who would utter any slight against her name. Whitlock's reasoning: "People do not consistently invite angry people into their homes."[2]

This protracted hullabaloo, which did not end with Whitlock's piece on Taylor, nearly runs the full gamut of issues explored in *On the Sidelines*.[3] From McNeil's slut-shaming comments on Taylor's MNF attire and Gottlieb questioning her knowledge of the NBA, to Whitlock reducing the availability of Taylor's opportunities to her appearance and making the racially coded recommendation that she ignore her detractors and not be so "angry," such are the contemporary experiences of women sportscasters in the United States. As I explain throughout this volume, these contemporary experiences have been largely wrought by gendered neoliberalism.

One can therefore surmise that Taylor's experience in 2020 was neither new nor isolated. Many of the women who fall into the category of "woman sportscaster" are perhaps excessively admired for their beauty, while also evoking considerable gendered and racialized scorn, as further demonstrated by the following flashpoints—all of which occurred within the span of four consecutive months in 2014.

Kirk Minihane, a sports talk radio host in Boston, referred to sideline reporter Erin Andrews as a "gutless bitch" for conducting what he believed to be a halfhearted interview during the Major League Baseball All-Star Game. He apologized a few moments later but not without stating that Andrews lacked talent and would be a waitress if she "weighed 15 pounds more" (Finn 2014).

In speaking about host and reporter Sam Ponder on a podcast, Dave Portnoy, the founder of blog *Barstool Sports*, said, "No person who watches [her show] wants to see a picture [on social media] of her and her ugly kid. . . . We want to see [her] sex it up and be slutty." Portnoy was defending sports blogs, which Ponder accused of being hypocritical in their analysis of the Ray Rice domestic abuse saga. According to Portnoy, sports blogs could justifiably objectify women sportscasters while also advocating against domestic violence (Abelson 2017).

Ponder and Portnoy's feud has resurfaced twice since 2014. First, in 2017, Ponder and other women at ESPN took issue with the sports network's partnering with Portnoy's company to create a new television show, *Barstool Van Talk*. The show lasted one episode before it was canceled. Second, in 2018, Portnoy called for his blog's zealous followers, known as "stoolies," to harass Ponder online after he accused her of fabricating certain comments Portnoy allegedly made about Ponder and her infant child during their initial debate in 2014 (Wagner 2018).

Last, in November 2014, white comedian Artie Lange posted a series of tweets that described, in explicit detail, a sexual fantasy in which he was Thomas Jefferson and Cari Champion, a Black woman and then-moderator of ESPN's *First Take*, was his rebellious slave: "I attempt to whip [Champion] cuz she disrespected the Jefferson Plantation but she grabs [my] whip & beats me I cum like a fat founding father" (D'Zurilla 2014).

As these flashpoints demonstrate, women in the electronic sports media industry often experience gendered mistreatment in the forms of humiliation, mockery, and online and offline harassment framed by (hetero)sexist and racist logic. In addition, these women are targeted not just by relatively anonymous sports media consumers but also by men who work within the sports and media industries and who have achieved varying levels of fame. The reasons for such attacks are multitudinous and contradictory; for some women sportscasters, their perceived attractiveness makes them objects of desire and targets of unsolicited remarks about their bodies and sexuality. For others, their attractiveness calls into question their credibility as sportscasters. Ultimately, all women sportscasters are vulnerable to this discourse simply because they are women.

The sexism that women in sports media encounter has not gone unnoticed by sports media scholars. A large body of scholarly literature has investigated, for example, the extent to which women in sports media face gendered double standards of appearance and sports knowledge (Harrison 2019; Sheffer and Schultz 2007) and gendered affective or emotional labor (Harrison 2018). Women sportscasters are also susceptible to visual objectification; as measured by eye-tracking technology, men and women television viewers' eyes tend to stray away from women sportscasters' faces and onto their bodies more often than they fixate on men sportscaster's bodies (Cummins, Ortiz, and Rankine 2018). Research has also found that sports media consumers hold sex biases in evaluations of sportscaster vocal tone (Etling et al. 2011) and authoritativeness (Etling and Young 2007). According to Daniel Davis and Janielle Krawczyk (2010), perceptions of woman sportscaster credibility are also positively correlated to perceived attractiveness. That is, as perceived sportscaster attractiveness increases, so does the perceived credibility of a woman sportscaster, *except* when a woman sportscaster is perceived to be *highly* attractive. In that case, a woman sportscaster's perceived credibility decreases.

Researchers have also found hegemonic masculinity to pervade materials used for both collegiate sports media instruction (Hardin, Dodd, and Lauffer 2009) and the industry itself (Bien-Aime 2016). Hegemonic masculinity is a subtle process through which men and women have come to view masculinity as an inherently natural trait throughout sport (Hardin and Shain 2006). There are five characteristics of hegemonic masculinity in mediated sport: physical force and control, achievement in the workplace, patriarchy based on a glamorizing of the traditional nuclear family, frontiersmanship, and heterosexuality (Trujillo 1991). The U.S. sports media (unintentionally) embrace these elements in its coverage of men's sports by presenting hegemonic masculinity as "common sense" while presenting those elements as "unnatural" for women's sports and women *in* sports. Although the current scholarly literature sheds light on the many sexist notions and practices that have been taken for granted throughout the sports media industry, it does not explain why or how these notions have come to exist, persist, and be taken as normal. This is the impetus for *On the Sidelines*.

Simply proving gendered inequities exist is not enough to curb them. Despite the scholarship at its disposal, the electronic sports media industry—as an amorphous, faceless entity—continues to be a problematic space for U.S. women in the early twenty-first century. As I argue throughout this book, the hostilities women face within this context persist because of a subjectivity, or an idealized notion of a female sportscaster, that is socially constructed through contemporary feminist discourses. Here, "contemporary feminism" encompasses postfeminism and neoliberal and popular feminism—together also known and henceforth referred to as "gendered neoliberalism" (Banet-Weiser, Gill, and Rottenberg 2019). This means that the idealized female sportscaster subject is someone who the industry and its consumers expect to be an always autonomous and entrepreneurial figure, capable of successfully navigating gendered barriers—such as sexual harassment—and persevering in the face of those barriers. These expectations are legitimized when the challenges women sportscasters encounter are seemingly solved by those women making choices they appear to be arriving at freely. When a middle-aged woman, as examined in chapter 1, makes changes to her wardrobe to appear "hot," and thus remain employed in an industry that privileges younger women, such a change can appear to be an act of free will. Instead, because of the threat of losing their positions to younger women and because of the backlash women often receive for showy wardrobe choices (exemplified by Dan McNeil's tweet), this is one of many lose-lose decisions women in the industry are forced to make, sometimes on a daily basis.

These choices are paradoxical, forcing women in the industry to adhere to a strict set of guidelines governing their behavior, temperament, and appearance but seemingly "empowering" them by placing the responsibility for their ability to exist within the industry squarely on their shoulders. That is, women in the industry are expected to navigate its gendered challenges with little to no meaningful institutional support, which contributes to the persistent and evolving marginalization of women in the industry. These challenges—and the sophisticated ways women are expected to autonomously grapple with them—are a symptom of a female sportscaster subjectivity that is constructed by contradictory and exclusionary gendered neoliberal discourses, many of which pervade the mass media landscape (Banet-Weiser 2018; Gill 2007; McRobbie 2004; Rottenberg 2018).

Of course, neoliberalism itself is central to the concept of gendered neoliberalism. On one hand, it calls upon women to constantly perform self-discipline and self-maintenance so they might thrive and succeed without statutory, institutional, or organizational assistance (Gill and Scharff 2011). On the other hand, neoliberalism also ignores—and, some might argue, relies on—the fact that certain individuals are disadvantaged, due to their social location (i.e., their race, gender, age, class, or [dis]ability). As a result of gendered neoliberalism's expectations of autonomy and a can-do attitude, the challenges women sportscasters face are taken for granted. "Of course she was harassed," many say. "She's a woman in a male-dominated industry!" The sports media industry is therefore absolved, theoretically, of any responsibility for the continued, systemic marginalization of the women it puts on the air.

This book and its findings will no doubt be met with some skepticism among the sports media industry's decision-makers, who often justify their (in)actions by taking certain phenomena, like sexism or their audience's desires, for granted. This is true whether these decision-makers answer questions about the lack of airtime given to women's sports (Cooky, Messner, and Musto 2015) or their justification for giving certain sports, regardless of gender, preferential television coverage over others (Saks and Yanity 2016). In short, to many of the industry's decision-makers—all of whom are tasked with turning a profit—my arguments may seem naïve. The issue of television ratings, which drive revenue within the television and radio sports industries, is not explicitly addressed until this book's concluding chapter. However, the purpose of *On the Sidelines* is to explain, in part, how the treatment of the industry's women sportscasters has been constructed to *appear* to be a natural consequence of the sports media enterprise. In other words, *On the Sidelines* attempts to show that the gendered mistreatment of women sportscasters is not "natural," that it is not the result of "boys being boys." In turn, I believe it to be unnecessary to view improving the treatment of women sportscasters as mutually exclusive of the quest for high television ratings. The industry can do both, if it wants to.

To arrive at these conclusions, I use an analytic approach rooted in the power/knowledge paradigm conceived by French social theorist Michel Foucault (1980, 1978) to analyze discourse that contributes to the production of a female sportscaster subjectivity. I call upon Foucault's work to serve as a compass for this project because he (like Stuart Hall and others) understood discourse—composed of language, images, texts, and practices—as inherently political, insofar as discourse is not simply a passive presentation of actions, facts, information, or entertainment but a producer of relations of power, dominance, and oppression between members of social groups. *On the Sidelines*, then, is an interpretation of the discourse that shapes and is shaped by the structures of power and oppression that govern both the idealized female sportscaster subject and the material experiences of "real-life" women sportscasters, who are tasked with navigating a quantitatively and qualitatively male-dominated industry.

The arguments made in the chapters ahead were constructed after conducting one-on-one telephone interviews with ten women sportscasters and four focus group discussions with men and women sports media consumers. In addition, a collection of nearly 150 relevant mediated texts—tweets, news articles, blog posts, and audio and video clips—was curated, analyzed, and put into conversation with the insights offered by my interview and focus group informants, with the observations of the sportscasters guiding the analysis of my findings. This book, then, is a culmination of an investigation of how the idea of the female sportscaster is constructed and known by society at large and how that constructed idea is brought to bear on the everyday lived experiences of women sportscasters and on the structure of the industry as a whole.

Gendered Neoliberalism in Sportscasting

As I stated previously, gendered neoliberalism's discourses inform the experiences of women sportscasters such that these discourses work to push women sportscasters toward autonomy and entrepreneurialism. In doing this, gendered neoliberalism absolves the industry of any responsibility for the treatment these women receive, reinforcing sportscasting's gendered toxicity. In this section I further explain the nuances of gendered neoliberalism—composed of postfeminism and neoliberal and popular feminism—within the context of U.S. sportscasting, priming the reader to explore the evidence I present in the chapters ahead.

As I define gendered neoliberalism, I follow the lead of British feminist theorist Rosalind Gill. She previously distinguished her usage of "postfeminism" as an "object of analysis," a phenomenon to be observed and critiqued, as opposed to a social movement or a time "after" feminism (Banet-Weiser, Gill, and Rottenberg 2019). I want to be clear, then, that gendered neoliberalism should also be understood throughout this book as a phenomenon to be critiqued. Therefore, not only is *On the Sidelines* a scholarly volume about women sportscasters in the United States; it is also a book about gendered neoliberalism and how it constructs idealized (and therefore exclusionary) identities. Further, this book illustrates the ways such idealized identities can impact the everyday experiences of women in Western, capitalistic societies in general and women in sportscasting in particular.

Postfeminism

Postfeminism is an integral component of both gendered neoliberalism in general and in the construction of the female sportscaster subjectivity specifically. Feminist theorist Angela McRobbie (2004, 255) defines postfeminism as "an active process by which feminist gains of the 1970s and '80s come to be undermined." It acts as an "undoing" of feminism, not purely by rejecting feminism's legitimacy as in a backlash, but by acknowledging—or "taking into account"—feminism's perceived success. This sophisticated undoing of feminism, "manifest in popular and political culture," pays reverence to feminism while also making it appear irrelevant, unsexy, and therefore no longer necessary despite its historic success (256). This process, a "double entanglement" of genuine feminist discourses with those that serve to reject feminism, has created a postfeminist media culture in which men *and* women, corporations, and states can produce discourse that undermines so-called second-wave feminism while that same discourse happily utilizes it (256). As a result of the proliferation of postfeminism and its continued presumption of equality between the sexes, postfeminism "provides a new horizon of power against which all sociological analyses must proceed" (McRobbie 2011, xi). Thus, any analysis of the "female sportscaster" must attend to the double entanglement—which is to say, the contradictory framing of women's empowerment—that postfeminist media culture sells.

Examples of postfeminism's double entanglement pervade the electronic sports media industry. As explained in chapter 1, in a seemingly feminist gesture when taken out of context, *Barstool Sports* founder David Portnoy called out sportscasting's gendered appearance double standard in 2014, but only for the purpose of weakening the feminist idea that women sportscasters should not be objectified. Since the industry places such a high priority on a woman sportscaster's appearance, Portnoy believes men are justified in ogling them. Similarly, Jason Whitlock used the existence of the appearance double standard in 2020 to delegitimize Maria Taylor's success. Furthermore, as discussed in chapter 3, criticizing a woman sportscaster's revealing on-air attire—a criticism rooted in second-wave feminism—is a strategy that can be used to undermine that sportscaster's campaign against issues that disproportionately affect women, like sexual harassment. This double entanglement is a contradictory yet sophisticated act of resistance against a proliferation of feminist voices and ideas in media culture and sportscasting. The contradictory nature of using feminist ideas to combat feminist gains therefore works to make feminism appear outdated. This process delegitimizes feminism and therefore reinforces the idea that issues such as objectification and harassment are "natural" and that women in the industry have no choice but to simply "deal with it." As I explain in chapter 4, the ideal female sportscaster is quite adept at performing the affective labor required to just "deal with it."

Rosalind Gill (2007, 1) expands on the notion of postfeminism as entanglement by proposing an examination of postfeminism as an object or sensibility because of a need to "hit the refresh key to explore how the media today construct femininity, masculinity and gender relations." Postfeminism as a sensibility is manifest in a variety of electronic and print media and is present in a series of recurring "themes, tropes, and constructions that characterize gender representations in the media in the early twenty-first century" (255). Along with postfeminism's double entanglement, many of these tropes—or "hallmarks," as Gill calls them—can be found not only in postfeminist media culture but also throughout discourse that constructs the female sportscaster subject.

For example, as explored in chapter 1's discussion on the industry's appearance double standard, there has been a noticeable turn for many women in the industry from passive sex object to "desiring sexual subject" (Gill 2007, 255). That is, instead of appearing to passively exist in the industry for the pleasure of men like David Portnoy, many women in the industry have taken to openly expressing their sexuality, presenting themselves more provocatively than women in the industry did before the turn of the century. Again, this appears to be a choice that women in the industry are freely making but, as I explain in chapter 1, it is not that simple. Women sportscasters are also susceptible to misogyny framed in irony and humor, another hallmark of postfeminist culture. After disseminating his tweets about Cari Champion, Artie Lange attempted to pass off his slave fantasy as a joke, proclaiming the ensuing outrage over his tweets as a symptom of a humorless "PC" culture. As explicated in chapter 3, this is a common tact men take after harassing women, and women sportscasters, online. The sexualization of women's bodies, messages of choice and empowerment, and a reassertion of "natural" differences between men and women are other postfeminist tropes that serve to paint a contradictory and exclusionary picture of an ideal female sportscaster subject who "chooses" to utilize her sexuality to overcome the "natural" disadvantages she faces in the industry.

These tropes therefore appear at various points throughout this book and contribute to exclusionary media representations of women that "coexist with stark and continuing inequalities and exclusions that relate to 'race'" and other markers of social identity (Gill 2007, 255). That is, like other mediated forms of representation of social identity, postfeminism does not work in a vacuum. In the case of the sportscasting industry, postfeminism intersects with race to construct the female sportscaster subject. As explored in chapter 1, the expectation is that the female sportscaster will exhibit white femininity at all times. This is not to say that the female sportscaster *must only* be white or that women of color are not permitted to live up to and embody this ideal. So long as they adhere to an Anglo-American brand of femininity that governs their appearance and comportment, women of color can also embody the female sportscaster subject. As Jess Butler (2013, 48) states, although postfeminism privileges white, middle-class, heterosexual women, "this does not necessarily mean that nonwhite, nonmiddle-class, and nonheterosexual women are altogether excluded from, or somehow unaffected by, postfeminist discourses." The impact of postfeminism on non-white women is that they are therefore expected to live up to a white feminine standard of beauty and behavior and, unsurprisingly, face misogyny *and* racism when they do not. Such was the case when Jason Whitlock, a Black man, warned Maria Taylor, a Black woman, to ignore her critics and avoid coming across as "angry" (Whitlock 2020).

The term *postfeminism* has encountered many contestations. Among them is the definition of the word itself. Some scholars, like Gill, have sought to define *postfeminism* as a critical object of analysis while others have defined it as a backlash to the second-wave feminism of the 1960s, 1970s, and 1980s; as a third wave of feminism; or as a time "after" feminism. Also up for debate is the question of whether and in what contexts the term should include a hyphen between *post* and *feminism*. I use the unhyphenated form of *postfeminism* to coincide with Gill's usage of the term. Indeed, it is her conception of post-feminism that is primarily referenced throughout *On the Sidelines*. In addition, and echoing Gill's definition of the term, "By forgoing the hyphen, [I] seek to credit and endow postfeminism with a certain cultural independence and critical history that acknowledges its existences as a *conceptual entity* and *analytic category* in its own right" (Genz and Brabon 2018, 25–26, emphasis in original).

Besides the politics of the hyphen, perhaps the biggest controversy surrounding postfeminism as an object of analysis is the legitimacy of the label itself, regardless of its hyphenation. The label's legitimacy has been questioned because it is based on the notion that postfeminism renders feminism as no longer relevant, a notion that scholars have found to be increasingly spurious in recent years. Although neoliberal and popular feminism also feature messages of women's autonomy, empowerment, and entrepreneurship, their break from postfeminism is based on a shift in popular and corporate culture—one that seemingly transpired while I conducted this research—that recognizes a need and a utility for feminism (even if that need and utility is cynical). Prominent examples include Gillette's 2019 toxic masculinity ad and the word *feminist* lit up behind Beyoncé as the artist performed at MTV's Video Music Awards in 2014. As was not the case in McRobbie and Gill's definitions of *postfeminism*, feminism is "cool" again. Not only have liberal women such as Beyoncé and Emma Watson openly professed to being feminist, but so have conservative women such as Theresa May and Ivanka Trump (Banet-Weiser, Gill, and Rottenberg 2019, 15). Likewise, corporations such as Gillette—known primarily for its men's grooming products—have come to understand that it may be profitable to champion feminist causes. In other words, as Catherine Rottenberg states, "We are experiencing a feminist renaissance of sorts" (16).

In the electronic sports media, we have seen a similar deployment of feminist discourses in both the coverage of women's sports and the presentation of women working in sportscasting. One only need to recall Katie Nolan's comedic sketch for her talk show on ESPN (2019) portraying a "secret society" of women working in sports media. Given these and other similar developments through media culture, Gill has acknowledged that the term *postfeminism* may be obsolete, even if the traits of that object of analysis are still very much in play. She has therefore come to believe "gendered neoliberalism" more accurately describes the phenomenon instead (14).

Neoliberalism and Neoliberal Feminism

Whereas postfeminism provides a lens of analysis through which we can parse out evidence of gendered neoliberalism in sportscasting, neoliberalism and neoliberal feminism act more as a thematic glue that holds gendered neoliberalism together. Neoliberalism, another term with multiple recognized meanings, is a political and economic structure that governs women in sportscasting, among other folk, hovering over the industry as a specter, shaping and informing the female sportscaster subject. As opposed to an analytical lens, and whereas postfeminist discourse is the mechanism through which the female sportscaster subject is constructed, neoliberalism is the sociopolitical structure that necessitates women in sportscasting adhere to that female sportscaster ideal.

Although neoliberal feminism has made feminism cool again, it is similar to Gill's postfeminism in that it calls on women to adopt a neoliberal mentality, to pull themselves up by their bootstraps and, in the words of Facebook Chief Operating Officer Sheryl Sandberg, "lean in" (Rottenberg 2018). Here, I refer to neoliberalism as a political and economic model in which "privatization, deregulation, and a rolling back and withdrawal of the state" serve to encourage individuals and organizations to embrace autonomy and entrepreneurialism (Gill and Scharff 2011, 6). Made most visible in the United States during the Reagan administration in the 1980s and evolved under the Clinton administration in the 1990s, neoliberalism stresses the "psychological internalization of individual [responsibility]." As a result, neoliberalism places the onus on individuals for their own success and survival while ignoring race, socioeconomic status, gender, (dis)ability and other social markers as possible structural barriers to success.

Neoliberal feminism acknowledges inequalities between men and women but, paradoxically, "offers no critique—immanent or otherwise—of neoliberalism or its rationality" (Rottenberg 2018, 54–55). This paradox persists because neoliberalism needs feminism. Economically, neoliberalism relies on "reproduction and care work" to maintain human capital, but politically, neoliberalism is incapable of valuing that same reproduction and care work since there is no tangible market for such work (Banet-Weiser, Gill, and Rottenberg 2019, 6). Neoliberal feminism, then, "construes women not only as entrepreneurial subjects but also as individual enterprises," while placing the onus for reproduction and care work squarely on their shoulders. The result is a discourse of balance, a rejection of the refrain that "women can't have it all."

On the Sidelines does not explore women sportscasters' quest for work-home balance. However, the concept of neoliberal feminism is apropos within this project because its essence, that women sportscasters are solely responsible for "leaning in" and overcoming sexism, pervades the media landscape, including the messages and assumptions that are commonly held within the electronic sports media industry. Among those assumptions is the notion that women sportscasters must have thick skin when confronted with gendered mistreatment, as explored in chapter 4. Rosalind Gill and Christina Scharff (2011, 1) have connected a thread through postfeminism, neoliberalism, and the social construction of subjectivities like "female sportscaster." This thread contributes to the coexistence of messages of women's and girl's empowerment with a "reinvigoration of inequalities and the emergence of new forms . . . of power." That is, postfeminism, neoliberalism, and subjectivities work together as a crucial component of the continued marginalization of women in a society in which media culture would have us believe that "making it" as a woman is solely dependent on one's attitude and perseverance. To be clear, a critique of neoliberalism and neoliberal feminism should not be read as a rejection of responsibility and perseverance. As humans, we learn at an early age that those values are indeed important in most facets of life. However, when an expectation of those values coincides with and legitimizes a failure to address social injustices, the concepts of responsibility and perseverance serve to maintain an exclusionary status quo.

Popular Feminism

Throughout *On the Sidelines*, I argue that although there now appear to be more women in the electronic sports media industry than there have ever been before, many structural barriers remain on the path toward true gender equality. The third and final component of gendered neoliberalism, popular feminism, offers another lens through which we can analyze this contradiction. Through the concept of popular feminism—on its own and in combination with postfeminism and neoliberal feminism—we are able to see that the growing number of women in sportscasting makes women more visible in sportscasting but does little to move the needle politically.

While it is an object of analysis, popular feminism, as its label suggests, is also a particular brand of feminist discourse that seeks to capitalize on feminism's popularity. It is not sufficient to say that these feminist discourses are now popular just because they have gained acceptance. Instead, feminism is now popular in at least these three respects. First, no longer exclusively the stuff of academia, feminism pervades the mass media landscape; second, feminism has found widespread admiration, enabling its proliferation in the mass media; and third, a number of distinct feminisms compete for visibility in the mass media (Banet-Weiser 2018, 1). This means that feminism has become part of an economy of visibility, where individuals and organizations fight to have their feminism—and women in general— seen, liked, retweeted, and shared (27).

Popular feminism's emphasis on visibility is problematic insofar as *being visible* is as far as popular feminism goes. It is a corporatized, "happy," and "media-friendly" feminism that obscures any real critiques of patriarchy and white supremacy, and it believes that, by making women more visible and giving them a seat at the proverbial table, feminism's problems will be solved (Banet-Weiser, Gill, and Rottenberg 2019, 7). Hollywood, for example, has seen this emphasis on visibility in the calls for more women film directors, and more women in leadership roles in general. Yet, despite a growing number of women helming films, the Ninety-First and Ninety-Second Academy Awards both saw zero women nominated in the best director category, despite a slew of worthy candidates (Lee 2019; Nguyen 2020). Similarly, despite the increased number of women anchors and reporters on highly visible platforms such as ESPN and FOX Sports, women are still not afforded the same opportunities to explore other roles, such as play-by-play announcing (chapter 2), and are still subjected to workplace and online sexual harassment (chapter 3). While its discourse is highly visible and while it makes women more visible, popular feminism does little to address and remove barriers that prevent true gender equity.

Among those barriers is a troubling trend that has grown in lockstep with popular feminism: popular misogyny, or a popularized hatred of women. Misogyny, like feminism, is not new, but it is now popular in the same fashion feminism has become popular (Banet-Weiser

2018). Popular misogyny "also circulates in an economy of visibility" but, unlike popular feminism, has been made more real and concrete by "institutions and structures" such as policies and rhetoric championed by U.S. state and federal governments, and the general sentiment that "boys will be boys" (32). That is, while popular feminism does little to move the political needle, popular misogyny does much more, as evidenced by the Trump administration's efforts to roll back Obama-era Title IX gender discrimination regulations, efforts that have been widely applauded by so-called men's rights groups (Perez and Quilantan 2020). Additionally, whereas feminism and its champions are more proactive and hypervisible in media culture, popular misogyny "is expressed more as a norm, invisible, commonplace"; it is reactive and benefits from the anonymity and isolation afforded by the online environment (Banet-Weiser 2018, 32–33).

The online environment, and the popular misogyny it breeds, has had an immense effect on the material experiences of women sportscasters. As part of its reactiveness, popular misogyny often mirrors discourses disseminated by popular feminism but, much like a funhouse mirror, does so in a way that distorts those discourses (Banet-Weiser 2018, 39). We have seen popular misogyny in the online harassment of women in male-dominated industries, such as the video gaming industry and the #Gamergate controversy (33). Likewise, women in the electronic sports media industry have suffered disproportionate online harassment. In chapter 2, I briefly explore popular misogyny as reactive to the gains women have made in becoming more visible in previously unattainable sportscasting positions. In chapter 3, I more specifically examine the online harassment of women sportscasters, as illustrated in explicit detail by the "#MoreThanMean" public service announcement. I argue that the reaction to that PSA in some circles resembles popular misogyny's funhouse mirror, distorting and satirizing its message. The irony of the relationship that exists between popular feminism and misogyny is that both necessitate the other's existence. As feminism has become more popular, misogyny has also grown louder—that much is obvious. What is less obvious is that, as misogyny has been popularized, the mass proliferation of feminist discourses has become more justified. Thus, the popularity of feminism has caused harassment such as that explored in "#MoreThanMean." However, the PSA also wrought a highly visible, misogynistic response. So the cycle continues.

When combined to form gendered neoliberalism, postfeminism, neoliberal, and popular feminism work together to construct—through discourse and structures of power—an idealized female sportscaster subject that takes responsibility for her own success by displaying "empowered" white, heterosexual femininity; by embracing the "natural" differences that make her goals, skills, and assets unique from those of her male counterparts; by managing her emotions and rolling with the punches wrought by sexual harassment and bias; and by making herself more visible, sometimes by expressing her (white, heterosexual) femininity more explicitly. In addition, the female sportscaster subject must do all of this while enduring contradictory criticisms. On one hand, there is a set of sports media consumers (men *and* women) that would rather see women sportscasters quietly stand *on the sidelines* and "look pretty" or, in the words of David Portnoy, "sex it up and be slutty." On the other hand, there is another set of consumers that would rather see women sportscasters focus less on their looks and more on delivering sports information. Not only do these criticisms contradict each other, but they contradict the basic assumptions we hold about the female sportscaster subject and the privileges we believe she is afforded as a result of her "empowerment." These contradictions show that women sportscasters do not really have choices and are not truly empowered; they are damned if they do and damned if they don't. Gendered neoliberalism is rife with such contradictions, and perhaps the most damning of them all is the fact that women who choose not to conform to neoliberal expectations—and therefore leave the industry—prove neoliberalism's necessity in this environment. After all, if they had only had "the right temperament" or had only put on "the right attitude" or otherwise conformed to gendered neoliberalism, they would still be in the industry. These contradictions impact the material experiences of women sportscasters; *On the Sidelines* is a deep dive into those experiences.

Operationalizing Terms

Suffice it to say the term *female sportscaster* is loaded with a slew of meanings and carries with it a set of assumptions regarding sportscaster gender that undergird much of the discourse analyzed in this volume. Although commonly used in media and everyday talk to refer to a woman who provides sports reporting and commentary through broadcast media, I use the phrase to describe a subjectivity or constructed identity. It is therefore important to specify when I am referring to this subjectivity and when I am writing about actual, corporeal women. *Woman sportscaster*, or its plural equivalent, is used to refer to the women who were interviewed for this project as well as those whose experiences can be found in media discourse. Not only do I use the term *woman sportscaster* to differentiate the real from the imagined in this book, but I use the word *woman* because it is less clinical and more inclusive than *female*. The word *woman* is more inclusive because not everyone who identifies as a woman is biologically female; it is not my intention to identify the women referenced in this book by their reproductive anatomy. Conversely, as a constructed, imagined subject, *female sportscaster* works because it carries with it a set of assumptions that include the expectation that "female sportscasters" are cisgender and heterosexual.[4]

For the purpose of this project, a woman sportscaster is defined as a person who identifies as a woman and appears on or is heard through a broadcast, cable, satellite, or digital medium to provide commentary or news about sports. Since most of these various types of media cannot be accurately described as broadcast media, for the sake of simplicity, I use *sportscasting* when describing the industry and the various media within which the women under study are employed.[5] The women who fall within the purview of this project are seen and heard through various platforms, including television and radio as well as the internet (i.e., podcasting), and hold various on-air roles within the industry, including reporter, anchor, host, moderator, and, to a lesser extent, play-by-play announcer, color commentator, and studio analyst.

Why *Women in Sportscasting*?

Much of the scholarship examining gender in the sports media industry does not differentiate between women sportscasters and women sports journalists, using *women in sports journalism* as a catch-all phrase that includes women who work in print *and* electronic media.

Although I call upon literature and mediated texts related to women in sports journalism collectively, this project focuses on sportscasters only. Within the sports media industrial complex, sportscasters are more visible than their counterparts in the print media. In the print media, the words on the page tell the story, whereas in television media, the sportscasters tell the story, leaving them more susceptible to (para)social interactions from the audience.[6] This distinction between sportscasters and print journalists is important especially as one considers the sorts of vitriolic online interactions that motivated sportscasters Julie DiCaro and Sarah Spain to collaborate on the "#MoreThanMean" public service announcement. Many of the comments curated for the PSA emphasized DiCaro's and Spain's appearance and vocal quality. I therefore concentrate on sportscasting as a site for examining gender in sports media, due to the lack of anonymity often afforded to sportscasters, relative to print journalists. Because of the variety of platforms through which sportscasters are now expected to appear, and as a result of the coincidental rises in popular feminism and misogyny, many of the obstacles women sportscasters must grapple with are a result of sportscasters' unprecedented accessibility and visibility.

The obstacles analyzed in this book (double standards, gender bias, and harassment) are not new but they are nevertheless worthy of examination now. As Dreama Moon (1999, 187) writes, "Once established, relations of domination do not persist on their own momentum but must constantly be reproduced in material and discursive ways." Thus, *On the Sidelines* is an examination of how gendered neoliberal discourse reproduces and sustains gendered relations of domination within sportscasting such as double standards, gender bias, and harassment. Since these phenomena are not unique to the sportscasting industry, this volume is therefore also an examination of the sports media industry as a gender*ed* space insofar as the heterosexism and racism that pervades society is brought to bear on the industry.

Conversely, this study also serves as an investigation of sports media as a gender*ing* space, an institution that *contributes* to our culture's heterosexism and racism as much as it is informed by it. The institution of mediated sport makes for a rich site of cultural inquiry because the institution is part of a social structure (in this case, and in short, patriarchy) that is not centralized but is composed of a network of connected institutions that equally contribute to the subjugation of women in society at large. Although it may appear that many of the phenomena analyzed in this book cannot be resolved unless they are addressed in society at large, the decentralization of heterosexism therefore means these interrelated institutions—which include mediated sports—must each take unique steps toward addressing socially embedded phenomena such as sex bias and harassment.

Women in Sports Media: Long-standing Trends

On the Sidelines attempts to take an underutilized approach to investigating a previously well-researched area of scholarship. In this section, I therefore contextualize and situate this volume within the body of knowledge that already exists vis-à-vis gender and sports media.

The Impact of Women's Sports Coverage

Women's sports have historically received coverage of lesser quantity and quality when compared to men's sports. Though I examine the plight of women sportscasters in this volume, the long-standing marginalization of women's sports and women *playing* sports has had an effect on women working in the industry. Despite the 1972 passage of Title IX, which has increased women's access to and interest in organized athletics (Cahn 1994; Garber 2002; Schell and Rodriguez 2000; Snyder 1993), women's sports remains on the periphery of the sports media industry and this marginalization has ramifications for women sports journalists.[7] Women's sports are given relatively little airtime (Cooky, Messner, and Musto 2015; Creedon 1994; Duncan, Jensen and Messner 1993; Eastman and Billings 2000; Tuchman 1979); there are a relatively small number of women in prominent sports media roles (Hardin and Whiteside 2006; "Richard Lapchick Study" 2015; Papper 2008; Sheffer and Schultz 2007); and sports journalists display an ambivalent attitude toward their desire to cover women's sports (Antunovic 2015).

In addition, women's sports television coverage is now subject to "gender-bland sexism" (Musto, Cooky, and Messner 2017), an uninspiring brand of coverage that uses lackluster commentary and low production values, which mark women's sports as inferior to men's sports. This sort of discursive practice, of (often unintentionally) implying inferiority through the usage of inferior production values, mirrors the discursive subordination of the sideline reporter position—a role in which women predominate. As noted in chapter 2, the sideline reporter position was initially held by a man and was created by the industry to offer non-serious commentary. Coupled with a prioritization of attractiveness in hiring for women sideline reporters, the non-serious nature of the role has resulted in the construction of a sports media personality whose perceived credibility is diminished.

The marginalization of women's sports has an effect on the experiences and attitudes of women sports journalists. Pam Creedon (1998, 95) refers to this marginalization of women's sports within journalism as being part and parcel of "the sports coverage hierarchy," which ensures women's sports and, by extension, women sports journalists remain ensnared in the sports media complex's hegemonic cycle. The sports coverage hierarchy rewards the best men and women sports journalists with men's sports assignments, which bring with them greater prestige and higher salaries. This system persuades the most ambitious sports journalists to gravitate toward men's sports, thus leaving women's sports—and women *in* sports—on the periphery.

Lesley Visser, former sideline reporter for CBS Sports, captured the spirit of the sports coverage hierarchy when she said: "Women who get into sports journalism don't want to cover women's sports. They want to cover sports that lead to success" (Cramer 1994, 169). Annette John-Hall, a former beat writer assigned to Stanford University athletics said, "If you want to succeed in sportswriting, you don't want to cover women's sports. Women sportswriters get pigeonholed into women's sports, and when that happens, your career stalls." Athletes notice this avoidance of women's sports by talented journalists as well. Cynthia Cooper, a former player in the Women's National Basketball Association (WNBA), once remarked, "I'm a pro athlete. . . . Why should I have to beg and plead for attention? I am so tired of ignorant journalists covering me. I'm so tired of [being mistaken for teammate] Cheryl Swoopes. How many NBA players have to deal with that?" (Creedon and Smith 2007, 149). Though these comments were made during the 1990s, they demonstrate a long-standing prioritization of men's sports, which has slowed the progress women have made within the industry. If, for example, women journalists wanted to cover men's sports during the 1980s and 1990s—a time when women were struggling to gain access to and acceptance in men's locker rooms and clubhouses—the sports coverage hierarchy served to ensure women would need to toil in some of the industry's most toxic environments to earn prestige and acclaim.

As women remain on the periphery of the sports media industry, it also becomes easier for some to justify their marginalization. The concept of symbolic annihilation (Gerbner 1978) has been used by scholars as a way of explaining the marginalization of certain news stories in general. If agenda-setting theory (McCombs and Shaw 1972) provides our understanding for how news story selection affects audience salience—that is, the media's story selection tells the audience what issues and events are most important—symbolic annihilation provides the opposite understanding. Sports media decision-makers often attribute the decision not to provide equal coverage for men's and women's sports to television ratings and print readership, which skew toward men's sports. Nevertheless, according to symbolic annihilation, by choosing not to cover women's sports prominently, the media implicitly tell the audience not to prioritize women's sports. Over the past three and a half decades, various scholars have put their scholarship in conversation with Gerbner's symbolic annihilation as a way of explicating the relative invisibility of women within the sports media industry (Cooky, Messner, and Hextrum 2013; Creedon 1994; Messner, Duncan, and Cooky 2003; Tuchman 1979).

Agenda-setting theory suggests that stories on the front page and above the fold of a newspaper are deemed more salient by the media and, therefore, by media consumers as well. Not only was the placement of women's sports above the fold rare in 1979, but also their newspaper coverage was inconsistent overall, contributing to their symbolic annihilation (Tuchman 1979). More than four decades later, the amount of women's sports coverage has not increased significantly. In a longitudinal study of women's sports coverage by television news outlets, three local newscasts as well as ESPN's flagship highlight show, *SportsCenter*, were found to have actually decreased the amount of time they devoted to women's sports over the previous twenty-five years (Cooky, Messner, and Musto 2015). While symbolic annihilation is not a guiding concept in *On the Sidelines*, the theory is nevertheless apropos here because it provides a lens through which we can understand the sportscasting industry's uneven representation of women. We can also consider agenda setting and symbolic annihilation's relationship to this Foucauldian project: if the presence of certain discourses can shape real-life experiences and subjectivities, logically, the absence of particular discourses could have a similar impact.

The relationship between power and knowledge and symbolic annihilation is especially apparent in chapter 2, in which I analyze a commonly held aversion to women's voices among many sports media consumers. This aversion, caused chiefly by a historic lack of women's voices on the air, illustrates the potential impact of long-standing symbolic annihilation. In this case, the discursive exclusion of women from certain sportscasting roles has made sports fans (men *and* women) less receptive to hearing women in those roles. In general, sports fans are not used to hearing women announce a game live. The taken-for-granted invisibility and rejection of women in sports—seemingly justified by the revenues generated by ratings and readership and the commonsensical notion that this is a "man's industry"—makes it difficult for many people, regardless of their gender, to envision a sports media industry in which men and women should be given equal consideration for roles in which they use their voices.

The Statistical Gender Disparity among Sports Journalists

Despite women's increased interest and participation in sports post–Title IX, the reality is that men still quantitatively and ideologically predominate sports. Thus, it is difficult to discern any sort of bias or other form of gendered mistreatment from industry statistics, and as a result, it is convenient to normalize such numbers as a natural consequence of the way men and women and boys and girls engage sports. Conversely, the numbers do not disprove the existence of gendered mistreatment, either. The stories reported by the popular press, and those told by the women I interviewed, offer evidence that gendered mistreatment is normalized in sportscasting, yet available statistics do not and cannot account for this. As I argue in chapters 3 and 4, the gendered mistreatment of women sportscasters—and the industry's lack of effort in addressing that mistreatment—play a large role in keeping many women away from the industry. Thus, while industry statistics showing gendered disparities may appear to be a natural consequence of the way women, men, girls, and boys have been taught to engage sport socially, so it is that the sports media industry has played an equal role in the perpetuation of the status quo. Discourse is the mechanism through which the status quo is maintained. Gendered neoliberal discourses—such as the idea that the gendered structure of the industry is "natural"—are what maintain the status quo governing women sportscasters in the contemporary moment.

What is the status quo? Although women can be seen in some of sports media's most prominent national television outlets, both on the sidelines (e.g., Erin Andrews, Pam Oliver, and Michelle Tafoya) and in the studio (e.g., Linda Cohn, Charissa Thompson, Maria Taylor), the proliferation of women at the national level of American sportscasting appears to be a false positive. Across the vast collection of U.S. local and national print and electronic media outlets, women make up a relatively miniscule portion of the sports media labor force.

The Institute for Diversity and Ethics in Sport (TIDES), in conjunction with the University of Central Florida, regularly conducts and publishes a diversity report card commissioned by the Associated Press Sports Editors (APSE). This report card measures the extent to which sports print media outlets are (or are not) becoming more diverse with regard to both race and gender. Although the TIDES report is solely focused on print sports media, it is nevertheless relevant as it serves as an example of the quantitative marginalization of women in sports media overall. As of their most recent report card (Lapchick et al. 2018), APSE newspapers and websites overall earned an F for gender diversity. This was the fifth consecutive report in which the APSE earned an F for gender diversity since the APSE began commissioning these reports in 2008. By comparison, APSE outlets earned a B+ for racial diversity, although, as noted in the report, that grade is largely bolstered by ESPN(.com)'s highly inclusive hiring practices (Lapchick et al. 2018, 3).

What does an F mean for the APSE? It means that women are not being hired by sports media outlets at a rate that is close, by any definition, to that of male sports journalists. Additionally, women continue to struggle to earn prestigious print journalism positions, such as columnist and sports editor, which TIDES's diversity grade calculations weigh more heavily. Overall, in 2018 women constituted 17.9 percent of sports print journalism staffs nationwide. Although this is a marked improvement on the 7.5 percent figure in the 2008 report card, there is still a discernible disparity in the number of men and women in print sports journalism.

The available television statistics are just as bleak: survey results released by the Radio Television Digital News Association (Papper 2008) found that only 7.8 percent of television sports anchors nationwide were women, while 18.7 percent of sports reporters were women. Although the results of this survey were released in 2008, this disparity further illustrates the long-standing marginalization of women in the sports media complex.[8] This especially rings true when one considers that in 2008, 56.8 percent of *news* anchors were women, which is representative of the current perception that most newscasts have one man and one woman anchor.

As it relates to job satisfaction, the existing statistical data paints an ambivalent picture, one in which women note the improvements made toward gender equity in sports journalism while also acknowledging that certain obstacles persist. This closely mirrors the overall impressions of the industry related to me by the sportscasters I interviewed. In a survey of 306 women sports journalists, Kimberly Miloch and colleagues (2005) found their respondents to have neutral feelings vis-à-vis job satisfaction. When separated by age, experience, salary, and job title, however, the feelings were divided. Those older than twenty-six, for example, reported fewer opportunities for entrance into the field, and women sports journalists who had less than six years of experience overall reported receiving more assignments specific to women's sports (227). This phenomenon tracks with Creedon's (1998) coverage hierarchy described previously. More prestigious and experienced sports journalists generally receive fewer women's sports assignments whereas women's sports assignments are often where younger, less accomplished women journalists "pay their dues." Unsurprisingly, women sports journalists earning below $35,000 annually perceived there to be fewer opportunities for advancement and more discrimination from supervisors than those with higher incomes (Miloch et al. 2006, 226).

The Starting Lineups

The following are the pseudonyms and backgrounds of the ten women interviewed for this project.

> Samantha, white, early twenties, an update anchor and self-described "girl voice" for a sports talk radio station in a large market in the western United States.

> Lizzy, white, late twenties, a fantasy sports talk-show host for a sports talk radio station in a large western market.

> Amelia, white, early forties, pre- and postgame show host and reporter for a regional sports television network (RSN) in a large western market.

> Nancy, white, mid-sixties, a semiretired reporter and host for an over-the-air national television broadcast network and its twenty-four-hour sports cable sister. Nancy is a member of the National Sportscasters and Sportswriters Association's Hall of Fame.

> Jane, white, late thirties, a freelance sports reporter often seen on an RSN in a large western market.

> Paula, Latina, early thirties, an Emmy Award–winning anchor and reporter for an RSN in a large western market.

> Stephanie, white, mid-twenties, self-identifying as queer, cohost and coproducer of a baseball podcast produced on the East Coast.

> Patricia, biracial, mid-twenties, a reporter and weekend sports anchor for a local television news station in a midsized eastern market.[9]

> Hannah, white, mid-twenties, a reporter for a local television news station and RSN in a small eastern market.

> Marie, white, mid-twenties, reporter and fill-in anchor for a local television station in a midsized eastern market.

The focus group participants, meanwhile, serve a function in this project that is similar to the mediated texts I have analyzed. That is, the media consumers in the focus groups should not be considered subject matter experts per se. Instead, they serve as a microscope of sorts through which we can view and analyze the effects of gendered neoliberal discourse on those who watch and listen to sports media content. These participants possessed the capacity to speak to some phenomena but not all. Thus, as this book moves toward analyses of the psychosocial impact of gendered neoliberalism on women in sportscasting, my usage of the focus group participants' insights necessarily decreases.

The arguments I advance in this book are presented across four chapters and a concluding chapter, "The Postgame Show." The first chapter examines the sports media industry's well-documented gendered double standards of appearance and credibility, and their most recent manifestations, through the lens of gendered neoliberalism. With regard to the appearance double standard, in true gendered neoliberal fashion, women sportscasters are presented with multiple predicaments that are contradictory and afford women in the industry few desirable options. One of these dilemmas is a trend I refer to as *nightclubification*, an increasing tendency among women sportscasters to wear revealing clothing. The nightclubification of women sportscasters' appearance is due in large part to an industry that has come to expect its women to comply with such a sartorial turn, an expectation and subsequent turn that has been both observed and documented by women throughout the sports and news media industries. In chapter 1, I also provide support for the argument that the electronic sports media's appearance double standard—and the female sportscaster subject—is constructed in large part by dominant notions of white femininity. These notions inform the standards of beauty and demeanor most often adopted by women sportscasters, regardless of their race. This undercurrent of Anglocentric white femininity therefore buttresses the gendered appearance double standard's status as the foundation upon which other forms of the industry's gendered mistreatment has been built. As it relates to the credibility double standard, which is informed by the appearance double standard, women sportscasters face gendered skepticism before they even have the opportunity to demonstrate their skills and knowledge and face unjust critiques after doing so. While the credibility double standard in and of itself is not representative of a gendered neoliberal subjectivity, the expectation that women navigate and overcome both double standards, with a can-do attitude and little to no institutional assistance, is very much rooted in neoliberalism and is taken for granted. As a result, although the existence of these double standards is well known, the sports media industry and its consumers have been slow to act against them.

Chapter 2 examines a gender bias in hiring for certain on-air positions in the electronic sports media industry, through the lens of gendered neoliberalism. Although there have been a few recent exceptions, such as Beth Mowins, Jessica Mendoza, and Doris Burke, women are largely excluded from television play-by-play announcing and color commentary positions for highly visible men's sports. This is symbolic of what I call sports media's "glass sportscasting booth," a site within sports media to which women sometimes aspire but are typically not hired. The chapter begins with an analysis of the position for which women *are* viewed as being ideally suited, the sideline reporter, since it offers us a glimpse of widely held perceptions of the role women sportscasters hold in the sports media industry. Chapter 2 then moves to an analysis of the lack of women assigned to the sportscasting booth as play-by-play announcers and color analysts for men's sports. My interview and focus group informants offered a variety of explanations for this phenomenon, ranging from the perceptions of women's voices to a lack of available qualified women play-by-play announcers and color commentators. In general, these explanations clarify the construction of a relatively narrow representation of women in sportscasting that ensures women's perceived inferiority in the industry now and in the foreseeable future. In addition, discourse that places the onus on women to access previously inaccessible roles—discourse to which many of my informants subscribe—is rooted in gendered neoliberalism. Lastly, chapter 2 explores popular misogyny's reaction to the relatively recent integration of women into the sportscasting booth.

Due in large part to the 2016 "#MoreThanMean" public service announcement, reports of the gendered harassment women sportscasters endure online have found a large audience.[10] On the other hand, mass mediated reports of workplace harassment in electronic sports media exist but have taken longer to find such an audience. Chapter 3 analyzes both forms of harassment in sportscasting. Regarding workplace harassment, women in the industry endure hostile work environments, stemming in part from the stigmatization of menstruation, pregnancy, and miscarriage. In addition to quid-pro-quo (or "this for that") propositions and stalking, the taboo surrounding female reproduction is informed by the double standards analyzed in chapter 1 and, by extension, women's perceived role in sportscasting as examined in chapter 2. Chapter 3 also examines the online harassment of women sportscasters through the lens of the online environment's role as an extension of a sportscaster's workplace (Laucella 2014). In chapter 3 I once again call upon popular feminism and misogyny to argue that woman sportscaster online harassment is a backlash to the increased integration of women in the electronic sports media industry. The online harassment of women sportscasters, undergirded by popular misogyny, serves to ensure the persistence of the gendered structure of the sports media industry, a structure in which women remain on the periphery. In a phenomenon that is a central component of the expectations of gendered neoliberalism, the harassment women in the industry endure—and the lack of action the industry has taken against it—forces women to discipline their actions so as not to invite unwanted advances or attacks.

In that vein, chapter 4 employs feminist affect theory to more closely examine the self-discipline that is required of women sportscasters in response to harassment, double standards, and gender bias. Using Sara Ahmed's (2014) work on affect as an entrée into Arlie Hochschild's (1983, 1979) concepts of emotional labor and emotion work, I explore the extra affective labor women sportscasters are required to perform in order to exhibit the unaffected demeanor the industry (and gendered neoliberalism) demands of women. For women in sportscasting, emotional labor is performed in the workplace in exchange for the sort of political capital that allows women sportscasters to gain influence in their media organizations. Emotion work, or emotion management that takes place outside the workplace, calls upon women sportscasters to seek interpersonal support that is often patronizing and normalizes the gendered mistreatment. Many women in the industry have persevered despite the expectation of emotion management while others have either left or have never entered the industry because the benefits of the job did not outweigh its emotional cost. This attrition further contributes to the gendered structure of the sportscasting industry. Additionally, and most relevant to my overall argument, the expectation of emotion management resonates with gendered neoliberalism's requirement that women discipline themselves and strive for success in the face of adversity.

"The Postgame Show" concludes this volume by moving away from my analysis of gendered neoliberalism in sportscasting to discuss the institutional and social implications of this book's arguments, with suggestions for making sportscasting more inclusive for women.

ONE

Postfeminism, White Femininity, and Sportscasting's Double Standards

Phyllis George died on May 16, 2020. George, who was crowned Miss America in 1971, became one of the United States' first women sportscasters when she was hired to cohost CBS's National Football League pregame show, *The NFL Today*, in 1975. Before her death, George was quoted as saying that being Miss America was "a help and a hindrance. . . . It [was] a help in that [it] opened doors." The hindrance for George was that she carried the "beauty queen" label with her throughout her sportscasting career and therefore "had to prove [herself] more than the next person" ("TV Pioneer Phyllis George" 2020).

George's entrance into the industry, both as a woman and as the winner of a beauty pageant, made a long-lasting impact on sportscasting that was brought to the fore at the time of her passing. On one hand, upon her death, many women (and some men) in the sports media industry publicly reasserted George's status as a pioneer for women in sportscasting (ESPN 2020). Several contemporary and former women sportscasters, including Beth Mowins (2020) and Lisa Guerrero (2020a), took to social media to offer their condolences and thanked George for paving their way into the industry. On the other hand, Guerrero later decried the often-sexualized representation of women sportscasters when she referenced an article that included her (and George) on a list of women sportscasting pioneers (Mead 2010). While almost all the women listed in the article were pictured either holding a microphone or sitting in a television studio, Guerrero's photo featured her posing for a men's magazine while wearing lingerie. "Interesting to see the pic they used of me after over a decade on the field covering sports," said Guerrero (2020b), who, as of this writing is an investigative journalist for the television show *Inside Edition*. "This is one of the reasons I'm glad I moved on."

Phyllis George's death, and the discourse immediately afterward, reminded us not only of the progress the industry made with respect to its representation of gender but also brought back into the spotlight some of the challenges women in the industry continue to face on a regular basis. Among those challenges is a pervasive emphasis placed on women's looks, a deeply rooted patriarchal practice reinforced by television networks initially hiring women like George who did not possess the typical credentials of a sports journalist. While men sportscasters earn points for being attractive too, the prioritization of appearance is disproportionately thrust upon women, representing a double standard that, as I argue in this chapter and throughout this book, serves as the foundation for all other obstacles women in the industry face. George's comment that she needed to prove herself "more than the next person" because of her status as a "beauty queen" is a microcosm of the analysis provided in this chapter.

Here, I approach the previously documented gendered double standards of appearance and credibility (Harrison 2019; Sheffer and Schultz 2007) as *the* point of departure for the construction of the neoliberal female sportscaster subjectivity. Unsurprisingly, my informants (both the women sportscasters and sports media consumers) and curated texts were in universal agreement: gendered double standards exist in sportscasting, defining a *double standard* as a rule or criterion that is applied differently to different people. In this case, men and women sportscasters are evaluated by superiors and media consumers differently across a variety of criteria, particularly those related to looks and perceived or assumed ability to perform the tasks typically assigned to a sportscaster. The existence of gendered double standards likely does not register as a surprise for most readers. However, the contemporary manifestations of those double standards are noteworthy here as they help illuminate the intricacies of gendered neoliberalism and its construction of exclusionary subjectivities. In that respect, these double standards are not unique to sportscasting but inform and are informed by much of the gendered neoliberal discourse that governs the experiences of women living in Western capitalistic nations. This discourse reinforces a set of boundaries and expectations that promote an exclusionary view of who is worthy of upward mobility, or in the case of sportscasting, who is worthy of going on the air. When it comes to sportscasting's gendered double standards, postfeminism (Gill 2007) is the predominant neoliberal discourse. Additionally, while postfeminism "isn't just for white girls" (Butler 2013), in sportscasting as in other arenas it does rely heavily on dominant ideals of white feminine appearance and temperament.

White femininity is an area of scholarship long studied by Black scholars but relatively new to a wider (and "whiter") swath of academia. The area of white femininity examines the normalization of white (cisgender heterosexual) feminine beauty and behavior and how that normalization serves our white supremacist patriarchy. White femininity appears normal—so it's the default femininity—and is constructed in a way that simultaneously privileges white women over women of color while also harming *all* women (Collins 2014; Deliovsky 2010; hooks 1990). Western culture's definition of what is beautiful changes over time, and we learn what counts as beautiful through images, not spoken words (Deliovsky 2010). In looking at media representations of women, Western culture's "patriarchal portrait" of the ideal woman is, among other things, "young, slim, tall, and cellulite-free with long, blonde hair, big (perky) breasts and blue or green eyes" that are constantly fixed on herself and on men (111). Behaviorally, a white feminine—and therefore "ideal"—woman is constantly nice, happy, smiling, nurturing, and deferential to men. Within the context of sportscasting, and as the examples provided in this chapter demonstrate, the previous physical and behavioral traits are part and parcel of the ideal neoliberal female sportscaster subject.

Women of Anglo-Saxon descent are most commonly blonde haired and blue eyed in North America and associated with purity and innocence, while women without these traits are often exoticized and associated with "sexual access and 'white' male pleasure" (Deliovsky 2010, 114). Although women of color are included in this exoticization, when they appear in the media, their appearance is often altered, either by themselves or by graphic artists, to be "whitified" or to more closely align with the ideal "white" traits listed previously. In sportscasting, for example, Black women sportscasters are expected to appear on air with long or straightened hair. As a result, hairstyles that are more commonly worn by women of African descent—hairstyles that feature shorter, tightly curled, or even braided hair—are rare in sportscasting ("The Internet Claims" 2018). These ideals are taught early in a woman sportscaster's development. Sonya Forte Duhé, the former director of the School of Communication and Design at Loyola University–New Orleans, reportedly told Black women broadcast journalism students that their otherwise "natural" hair should be straightened, while Duhé also showed "affinities for . . . the image of white, blonde hair, blue eyed anchors" often seen on conservative news outlets (Myskow and Hansen 2020). As another example, during a Q&A after a research talk, a Filipino woman admitted to me that when she was a teenager and aspired to be a sportscaster, her parents, believing she did not look like a sportscaster, encouraged her and financially supported her undergoing extensive hair treatments to "whitify" her appearance.

White femininity's "patriarchal portrait" is relevant to this chapter's analysis as it helps us understand why the expectations for sportscasting's gendered double standards are what they are. If Anglocentric notions of beauty and temperament are normative—such that they are the standard of appearance and comportment that *all* women are held to—then they should be (and are) apparent in both double standards. With respect to appearance, women sportscasters are expected to maintain a whitified appearance, at least presenting with a thin figure and long, straight hair. White femininity's boundaries for comportment command that women sportscasters should expect skepticism that they can perform the duties required of sportscasters. After all, the ideal (white) female sportscaster should not ask probing questions, should be deferential to her male colleagues and sources, and should be too focused on maintaining her appearance to hone her journalistic skills. As these criteria for ideal female sportscaster beauty and behavior privilege white women, it stands to reason, then, that gendered neoliberalism, the mechanism that normalizes these expectations in sportscasting, not only serves heterosexism and patriarchy but also white supremacy. The double standards analyzed in this chapter are therefore gendered *and* racialized.

Taken together, and as I argue throughout this chapter, neoliberalism broadly and postfeminist discourse specifically—both supported by the normalization of white femininity—serve to reinforce sportscasting's double standards of appearance and credibility. As I analyze ahead, the gendered and racialized appearance double standard is manifest in sportscaster hiring and retention, contradictory evaluations of a woman sportscaster's looks, and a phenomenon I call the *nightclubification* of woman sportscaster dress, evidenced by a drastic (and postfeminist) stylistic turn taken by sports television anchor Linda Cohn. Additionally, a brief analysis of sideline reporter Erin Andrews's career arc illustrates the positive and negative impacts for women who embrace the appearance double standard. Later in the chapter, I examine the credibility double standard, which manifests itself in assumptions of woman sportscaster promiscuity, gendered skepticism of a relatively unproven women sportscaster's skills and knowledge, and reactions to women who provide sports-related opinions on the air and online. The appearance double standard provides the foundation of the ideal neoliberal female sportscaster subject, making it the ideal topic on which to begin my analysis.

Appearance Double Standard

Hiring and Retention

Sportscaster hiring and retention is one of the most well-documented manifestations of sportscasting's appearance double standard. The appearance double standard's presence here establishes a baseline expectation that women aspiring to enter the industry must achieve, in neoliberal fashion. That is, aspiring women sportscasters must recognize this double standard and work independently to "overcome" (read: conform to) the disproportionate expectations of appearance that are placed on them. Additionally, though this manifestation is widely acknowledged, the industry has done little to meaningfully address it.

A survey of television news producers found that those who hired women sportscasters prioritized their attractiveness over their sports knowledge (Sheffer and Schultz 2007). The ten women sportscasters I spoke with were nearly unanimous in their assessment of this phenomenon, at least to the extent that appearance was not a criterion that was as prioritized in the hiring of male sportscasters. "Like, a better-looking guy doesn't really get the job," said Lizzy, a radio personality. "That isn't as influential for men as it is for women. And that's unfortunate but it's the truth." Similarly, ESPN personality Sarah Spain writes about the role appearance plays in the sportscasting industry, "We don't need our male sports reporters to be good at their jobs AND eye candy, they're allowed to just report" (2015, para. 6, emphasis in original). *Barstool Sports'* David Portnoy (2014, para. 3) wrote that ESPN's "Sam Ponder has a job because she's hot. Is she good at it? Can she think on her feet? Does she know sports? Probably but she doesn't even get in the door for an interview at ESPN if she doesn't look [the way] she does. It's requirement #1 for female sideline reporters."

Many of my focus group informants, including Molly, an undergraduate sports media student, agreed that looks are disproportionately prioritized for women sportscasters, even though, like most sports media consumers, she is not privy to the hiring decisions made within the industry. "Looks is such a huge factor. Any type of broadcasting, I believe that looks are a—it's sad to say, but [heterosexual male sports fans] want someone that's good-looking on TV, for sure." Marcus, an undergraduate studying business, offered this comment in support of the notion that appearance is of greater import in the hiring of women sportscasters than it is in the hiring of men: "It's that kind of thing that makes me think that it's more of an uphill battle for women. . . . Men—any of us—I feel like any of us would have a higher likelihood [of getting hired] if we just knew the right people and knew what we were talking about. Whereas, if a woman [had] all of that, [but wasn't] genetically born with the looks that society deems worthy, then their already-slim chances of getting there in the first place just becomes almost nonexistent."

When sports media professionals and consumers, men and women, are able to articulate these perceptions of the appearance double standard, the phenomenon has been taken for granted as common sense, even as standards of (white) feminine attractiveness are ever evolving. It is simply "known" that the female sportscaster *must* be "attractive" to enter and thrive in the industry. This knowledge—in which a norm has become normative and in which attractiveness becomes a form of power and oppression—therefore limits which women can be sportscasters.

Two of the sportscasters I spoke with, Nancy and Patricia, both believed attractiveness is also a consideration when directors and producers hire men sportscasters. However, the difference between the priority of appearance for men and women in the industry lies in the varying degrees to which attractiveness is prioritized in hiring men and women. This is not to say that *all* women sportscasters are universally attractive or even look like Deliovsky's (2010) white, "patriarchal portrait." Attractiveness is subjective, and many women sportscasters, like Michele Tafoya and Holly Rowe, are known more for their ability and professionalism than their looks. However, the perception among observers is that high levels of attractiveness is *the* consideration for women in the industry while it is *a* consideration for men. As is a common thread throughout this volume, this perception has a material impact on the experiences of women sportscasters that it generally does not have on men sportscasters. In that respect, one only need to revisit David Portnoy's (2014) comment that attractiveness is "requirement #1" for women sideline reporters and that this requirement justifies the pervasive objectification of women sportscasters.

The gendered and racialized double standard and prioritization of appearance over skill becomes even more apparent as sportscasters age. Recently retired play-by-play announcer Verne Lundquist called the Southeastern Conference's nationally televised college football game of the week on CBS until the age of seventy-six and, although Lundquist was recognized as having one of sportscasting's most recognizable voices, he was also portly with white, thinning hair. Along with his age, his physical traits are among those that women sportscasters are generally not afforded the opportunity to exhibit. The sixty-two-year-old, balding Tony Kornheiser, in a public apology after questioning the wardrobe choices of colleague Hannah Storm on his radio show, stated, "I'm a troll; look at me. I have no right to insult what anyone looks like" (Kennedy 2010, para. 9). ESPN personality Bomani Jones (2017), thirty-six years old at the time, professed his privilege as a man in this regard, tweeting: "I'm the skinniest dude in the world with a messed up [set of teeth] and hairline AND THEY PUT ME ON TV. Think about that" (emphasis in original). This is not to say that men are free to stay in the industry or in highly coveted positions for as long as they want, either. Some, such as Brent Musburger, who was at one time ABC/ESPN's lead college football play-by-play announcer, are demoted or forced out of their roles as they age. However, the discourse suggests that this attrition is more pronounced—and generally at an earlier age—among women and has more to do with appearance than it does for men.

The most important aspect of the hiring and retention manifestation of the appearance double standard is the extent to which it has been normalized. Without the double standard's normalization, neoliberalism has no basis for demanding women "deal with" this inequity. My informants' comments—and those made by sports media personalities in mediated texts—reveal a willingness, even if they are women who are already in the industry, to readily accept this hiring practice as a taken-for-granted and unbreakable reality. Jane, a freelance television reporter in her late thirties, also revealed such a willingness, despite stating, "Sadly, it's probably the part I don't like about my industry." As Kornheiser and Jones have demonstrated, men are also willing to accept this practice, implicitly and explicitly acknowledging that it is "normal" for men who are self-proclaimed "trolls" to be given the opportunity to provide sports commentary on television. The appearance criteria for men sportscasters are therefore incongruous to those for women. Further, this incongruity seems to be visible yet normal, insofar as many acknowledge it without calling for change or offering solutions to that effect. Gendered neoliberalism therefore tasks aspiring women sportscasters with overcoming this disadvantage with little to no meaningful support from the industry. Further, since most women who do successfully enter and thrive in the industry successfully navigate these expectations as they acknowledge them, neoliberalism demonstrates its own necessity.

Paradoxical Evaluations of On-Camera Appearance

The gendered and racialized appearance double standard is of course not confined to sportscasting's hiring practices; the phenomenon continues, in contradictory fashion, when women sportscasters appear on camera and are evaluated by the audience and industry decision-makers. It is also at this point that the neoliberal maintenance of the appearance double standard, as well as the construction of the female sportscaster subject, begins to rely heavily on postfeminist discourse and its attendant contradictions.

Many of the women sportscasters I interviewed expressed being scrutinized for their looks more often—and in greater detail—than their male counterparts. Patricia, the biracial anchor and reporter in her twenties, recalled the many times her station tweeted a photo of her and her colleagues previewing an all-woman newscast. Responses to the tweets often enumerated the differences in the broadcasters' bodies, especially if they wore similar clothing. "If it was two men wearing the same suit, everybody knows that that wouldn't be the case and that those comments wouldn't be thrown around," she said.

This emphasis on—some might even call it an obsession with—critiquing the bodies of women who appear on camera is a symptom of one of the hallmarks of Rosalind Gill's (2007, 255) postfeminist discourse, "femininity as a bodily property." In the age of pervasive gendered neoliberalism, a woman's perceived worth is often correlated to her possession of a "sexy" body. This correlation has led to the constant surveillance of women's bodies by media consumers, both men *and* women, and media organizations such as magazines, which often print large photographs of celebrities in swimsuits and critique their bodies. This obsession with women's bodies marks them as "always already unruly and requiring constant monitoring, surveillance, discipline and remodeling."

According to Patricia, media consumers often comment that she and certain of her women colleagues are either "too fat" or "too skinny." Comments like these act as a disciplinary mechanism through which the bodies of women on television are surveilled, calling on these women to constantly subscribe to a narrow, white feminine ideal. Further, subscribing to that ideal requires women to essentially defer to men and keep their eyes fixed on themselves in order to monitor their appearance. The expectation of self-surveillance, and the normalization thereof, is not new in the age of gendered neoliberalism. The contradictions within which that self-surveillance resides *are* unique to the contemporary moment, however, and further complicate the present emphasis on women's bodies.

That is, when it comes to maintaining an "ideal" body, women sportscasters are damned if they do and damned if they don't. As a result, the self-surveillance postfeminism requires of women sportscasters results in modes of self-presentation that are appealing to some and distasteful to others. Patricia stated she and her colleagues receive many critical emails whenever they wear red lipstick or certain dresses. Even though her news director approves of their stylistic choices, a sign that they are probably appropriate for some consumers, the women at Patricia's station often get emails in which viewers tell them "we look slutty, we look like whores." This paradox was also apparent when then-ESPN reporter Erin Andrews participated in *Dancing with the Stars* as a contestant in 2010. Reacting to a dress Andrews wore on the show, Elisabeth Hasselbeck, a then-host on the all-women roundtable morning show *The View*, questioned the appropriateness of the dress, slut- and victim-shaming Andrews, who had previously been stalked and secretly recorded in a hotel room (Everett 2010). After stating that Andrews wore "next to nothing," Hasselbeck said, "I mean, in some way if I'm [Andrews's stalker], I'm like, 'Man! I just could've waited 12 weeks and seen this—a little bit less—without the prison time!'" (Everett 2010, para. 7).

Women sportscasters have been increasingly expected to wear revealing outfits, as do competitive dancers, normalizing dresses such as that worn by Andrews. This paradox, in which industry norms clash with the tastes of a certain subset of the media consumer base, places women and women sportscasters in a double bind. Women in sportscasting must weigh the industrial rewards of wearing revealing clothing with the punishment society doles out as a result of such sartorial decisions. Given Daniel Davis and Janielle Krawczyk's (2010) study on women sportscasters' appearance, in which women who were deemed "least attractive" and "most attractive" were perceived as having less credibility than a woman in the middle of a predetermined "attractiveness" spectrum, it stands to reason that perceived women sportscaster credibility overall suffers as a result of industry norms and the paradox within which these norms reside. Hasselbeck's victim- and slut-shaming, and that endured by Patricia and her colleagues, is also an example of postfeminism's "entanglement" of feminist (*women should not be expected to dress like that*) and antifeminist (*no wonder she got stalked*) discourses (Gill 2007; McRobbie 2004). In this entanglement, media outlets and media consumers often co-opt feminist discourses to advance antifeminist arguments.

In addition to being paradoxical, the comments Patricia receives as a biracial woman, especially those that mention her hair, illustrates the appearance double standard's reliance on Anglocentric notions of femininity. "Viewers will call me Beyoncé or [say] 'your big hair this, that, and the other thing,' which they obviously would never [say] to a man, and also would never [say] to my blonde, white coworkers." Patricia also stated that most of the scrutiny she has received about her hair, makeup, and clothing comes from women viewers. In her memoir, ESPN anchor Linda Cohn (2008) wrote about criticism she received when *SportsCenter* began employing "tower shots," or camera angles that require the anchors to stand in front of a wall or large screen. As a result of this new angle, Cohn's wardrobe became heavily scrutinized by the show's producers and viewers, many of whom were women: "It seemed that over the next few months I was frequently being told I couldn't wear certain outfits because they were too tight, too revealing, or inappropriate" (ch. 10, para. 7). Cohn also detailed the scrutiny she received from women viewers, including an angry voicemail she received from a concerned mother, berating her for what the mother believed to be a stance that was too wide for "young boys' eyes" during a tower shot (para. 9). Andrews's, Cohn's, and Patricia's experiences all suggest women are also complicit in sportscasting's appearance paradox. As a matter of Foucauldian discourse, then, we can understand the woman sportscaster appearance double bind—one of many contradictions explored in this book—to be a result of a complex set of normalized ideas, practices, and images, and not monolithic, unilateral proclamations made by men.

The issue of makeup and hair is also part of this double bind. The women sportscasters I spoke with face criticism when they do not apply makeup. For example, TV anchor Marie stated that on days when her schedule is full and she has little time to do her hair or makeup before going on air, she will face criticism whereas, in the same circumstance, her male colleagues and superiors will not. "I had six and half minutes to get ready and people—I guarantee you that if my boss were to rush on set, his tie might not be completely done, people wouldn't say anything," she said. "For me, I'm going to get an email." Although she has not experienced this scrutiny, Hannah, an anchor and reporter, supported the assertion that a lack of hair and makeup preparation causes undue criticism by recalling some of her female colleagues' experiences. "If they weren't to wear makeup, [viewers would] say, 'Oh, this one looks tired. Why is she tired? I don't want to look at someone tired on my broadcast. This is ridiculous.'" Hannah also agreed that men do not receive equal criticism for their clothing. "No one would say, 'That guy's tie is too bright. That's too much. His suit is offending me.'" Marie and Hannah may be overstating their assertions by suggesting that "no one" would make these comments to men. However, considering the available media products and my informant's observations, we can surmise that women at least receive more of this sort of criticism than do men. Further, when women receive this criticism, it is often postfeminist, and therefore neoliberal, in its contradictoriness.

The Nightclubification of Women Sportscasters

Exacerbating the contradictory nature of the appearance double standard is a relatively recent turn in woman sportscaster dress that leans toward revealing, form-fitting clothing that had been previously reserved for nights out on the town. First emerging at the turn of the twenty-first century on conservative cable news network FOX News—and dubbed the *Foxification* of newscaster appearance—*nightclubification*, the term I use to describe the trend of wearing more revealing attire, has infiltrated sportscasting as well. As this aesthetic first appeared on a conservative U.S. television network, it should be unsurprising that it privileges women who demonstrate an exaggerated adherence to Anglocentric femininity. That is, women who were white, blonde haired and blue eyed, thin, and willing to show arms, shoulders, legs, and cleavage—and were deferential to (white) men—were given prominent airtime on FOX News at the turn of the century, and still are in 2020. Although this contemporary white feminine look has become normalized in sportscasting, it is a style that is still viewed as distasteful by many, including some women working in the industry. Nightclubification's contradictions, and its dubious status as a choice that women appear to be making freely despite the criticism it fosters, therefore inform the neoliberal discourse governing women sportscasters in the contemporary moment.

As the expectations of women sportscaster dress have become more risqué, the expectations placed on men sportscasters remain relatively conservative. Marie and Hannah's examples of male sportscaster criticism focused on men's sartorial choices—ties and suits—not their hair or makeup. In general, Western men, especially those who hold public-facing jobs, have fewer choices and therefore fewer expectations for hair and makeup, the latter of which men are generally not expected to use unless they appear on camera. This paucity of options and expectations for men is a deeply rooted reality that transcends sportscasting and results in hair and makeup being of greater import to a woman's overall attractiveness than it is for men. "It's sort of how it is," Amelia said. "It's just like if I go on a date with my husband, it might take me thirty minutes to get ready. It might take him two." Nevertheless, Marie and Hannah's claim that men and women are held to different standards when it comes to clothing is supported by my other informants and by stories found in the popular press.

The late Craig Sager, courtside reporter for the NBA on TNT until his death in 2016, was known for wearing suits and ties with loud colors and patterns. My focus group informants saw Sager's suits as a bit of a running gag. "The way he dressed, people loved it and it was fun to watch him. I don't know, it just made me laugh," said John, a male undergraduate. Marcus believed that a woman sportscaster with a similar fashion sense would not be so well received: "If a woman [wore] a flamboyant outfit, I think it would've been received less comically and more seriously and in a negative way, rather than a positive way. That was [Sager's] gimmick after a while. He would wear these suits—I think he was wearing them on purpose because it was his thing. But a female doing that long enough—she would never be employed long enough for that to become a thing."

Unlike the serious and often misogynistic evaluations of dress women sportscasters often experience, as John and Marcus suggest, the evaluations of men sportscasters' clothing often take a more lighthearted approach. *Esquire* included Sager in a story titled "The Long, Sordid History of Horribly Dressed Male Sportscasters" (Vinciguerra 2016). A closer look reveals the article—or, at the very least, its headline—was ironic, insofar as it reviewed and historicized, rather than critiqued, men sportscaster dress. The subheadline was "We can only assume LSD was involved," an attempt at humor to suggest drug use led to the sartorial choices of the men included in the article. Also, and more germane to the argument advanced in this chapter, the article explains the decision to dress eccentrically as a pragmatic one for male sportscasters who have sought to distinguish themselves from the rest of the crowd (para. 6), similar to Marcus's assessment of Sager's wardrobe. ABC's *Wide World of Sports* sportscasters wore bright yellow sports coats to distinguish themselves, for example. This attempt at standing out was made despite it rankling ABC's sports director at the time, who remarked that the coats "look[ed] like a fucking canary" (para. 11). Thus, men sportscasters *have* worn clothing to attract attention but, unlike their women colleagues, men sportscasters have rarely, if ever, felt it necessary to wear *revealing* clothing. Indeed, many women in electronic media industries have felt a need to do so in order stay on par with other women in the industry. Conversely, some women have been explicitly told by their superiors to don clothing that is less conservative, calling into question the notion that women have adopted this turn willingly.

Beth Teitell (2017) of the *Boston Globe* reported that women in the television news industry (which also includes sports and weather) have been increasingly told by their superiors to wear outfits that are more revealing. Teitell's story was spurred by the sudden retirement of Boston-area television news anchor Heather Unruh, who, upon retiring, stated, "Women are encouraged to dress more provocatively than I feel is appropriate for delivering news" (para. 2). Upon further investigation, Teitell found that the pressure women in the industry feel to dress sexy has become pervasive. As one anonymous newsperson told Teitell, "management at her station has told women to wear 'tighter, smaller, shorter, more revealing clothes'" (para. 4). Another woman newscaster referenced in the story reported occurrences of women affixing clothespins to the backs of their clothing to make it tighter and more revealing (para. 5), while another recalled her station's management asking her to dress more like her colleague who "wore her skirts short and her tops unbuttoned" (para. 8). The result is an environment in which many women in news and sportscasting, like the men sportscasters referenced previously, consciously wear clothing that will get them noticed (para. 9). The difference, however, is men in sportscasting do not feel it necessary to show more of their bodies.

The increase in revealing clothing appears to have created a race among some women in the electronic media industries to show the most skin their audiences will allow. This race, encouraged by managers who force otherwise unwilling women to do the same, has subjected women in the industry to the analogy that they are dressing for nightclubs. This analogy appeared in multiple texts I analyzed (Copeland 2013; Teitell 2017), as well as in some of the insights offered by my informants.

Although none of the women sportscasters I interviewed reported being asked by their superiors to dress less conservatively, many of them have noticed the trend toward more revealing clothing and lamented this shift. Paula, the Latina reporter and host, spoke the most passionately about the topic. "They're starting to dress women super inappropriately, like we're going to a damn club," she said. "If you go turn on FOX [Sports], ESPN, they're showing their legs, their arms, cleavage. It's a little over the top." Paula's comment seems to suggest that the women she sees may be instructed to wear revealing clothing. Samantha also noticed the trend. "I watch *SportsCenter* every morning. . . . Those girls . . . look like they're going to a nightclub, and so they have these dresses on and high heels and sometimes I wish that it would be more about what they're talking about and not just so much sex appeal." Marie expressed similar sentiments. "I personally look at [what others wear] and I'm like, 'That sure looks uncomfortable. I'm sorry you have to do that,' but that's their own choice." Marie's statement suggests that the women sportscasters she recalled willingly chose to wear revealing clothing.

Indeed, every woman in sportscasting nominally has a choice when it comes to clothing. For the women whose managers want them to adopt a more revealing style, however, the choices create another neoliberal double bind: wear revealing clothing while potentially subjecting themselves to the sort of slut-shaming referenced by Patricia, or dress conservatively and risk being passed over for promotion (or possibly replaced) by someone willing to show more skin. In Teitell's (2017, para. 9) *Globe* article, one newscaster spoke of her station's management hiring wardrobe consultants who recommended more revealing clothing, while another said they were pulled into a news director's office and reprimanded for wearing a jacket that was "too boxy." This newscaster also said, "This is so murky, because appearance is part of your job. [News executives] can be very subjective about how you move up and down the ladder" (para. 12). During a 2018 interview for HBO's *Real Sports with Bryant Gumbel*, NBA analyst Doris Burke admitted that, in order for her to make the switch from solely covering women's basketball to also covering men's professional basketball, ESPN required her to see a wardrobe consultant who would help her adopt a more stylish (read: form-fitting and revealing) style of dress.

With job offers, promotions, and higher salaries at stake, the nightclubification double bind creates an illusion of choice, especially for women who have spent time and money in college learning how to be sportscasters, a job whose number of opportunities is outstripped by its number of qualified candidates. If women adopt a revealing style of dress, they risk harassment and diminished perceived credibility. If they dress conservatively, they risk losing their jobs. As neoliberalism necessarily privileges those who are employed and upwardly mobile—after all, the more income you earn, the less assistance you require from the state—and marginalizes those who are not, it therefore encourages women to adopt a revealing style in this case. Thus, the choice many women sportscasters have isn't much of a choice at all. In general, the illusion of choice, a hallmark of postfeminist discourse, is exclusionary to the extent that the choices gendered neoliberalism "empowers" women to make regarding their appearance almost always call on them to emphasize ideal standards of (white) femininity (Gill 2007, 260).

Sarah Spain (2015, para. 6) hinted at the nightclubification double bind women sportscasters often encounter when she wrote that her first on-camera job

> was an incredible opportunity to work with big producers on a high budget and the only drawback was I had to wear low-cut shirts while I delivered fantasy football news. When you're just starting out and you don't know any better, you take a great opportunity when it's in front of you. When no one will give you a break and then a big-time producer hires you and you get to write the content and host and you just have to "be hot" like every other woman you see in the industry, then you think "I guess this is how the industry works" and you do it.

Spain has been slut-shamed online for her early-career wardrobe, even years after taking a turn toward more conservative attire. In chapter 3, I return to the case of Sarah Spain and the harassment she has endured as a direct result of her early-career attire.

The (Self-)Presentation of Women Sportscasters as Desiring Sexual Subjects

The need to wear more revealing clothing perhaps explains a turn taken by Linda Cohn. When Cohn's tenure at ESPN began in 1992 (at the age of thirty-two), she primarily wore loose-fitting pantsuits. However, as Cohn remained employed into her fifties and through her sixtieth birthday in 2019, the *SportsCenter* anchor's clothing became increasingly revealing, and a look at her Twitter account suggests the turn was intentional. On November 25, 2017, her profile picture was an image of her at a gym, bent over at the waist, looking at the camera as she posed with her hands on a balancing ball, with her hair down. Leaving her hair down in this context, while apparently working out, suggests the photo was staged. Cohn was also wearing spandex that stopped above the knee and a purple tank top, which, due to her posture, revealed her cleavage. On March 25, 2016, Cohn tweeted a photo of herself in which she was wearing a form-fitting dress and was turned with her side to the camera and her hands on her hips. It was clear that she disseminated this photo as a means of selling it; while including a link to purchase her autographed photos, she wrote, "This one is the top seller so far. Do you agree?" (Cohn 2016). On December 4, 2014, Cohn tweeted, "At least [co-anchor David Lloyd] was hard at work during a commercial break. I felt compelled to strike a pose" (Cohn 2014). With that tweet, Cohn included a photo of herself in one of the two *SportsCenter* anchor chairs, with her back to the desk and Lloyd in the background. She wore knee-high boots and a form-fitting, low-cut dress that stopped mid-thigh. Her tweet indicated that her pose and facial expression were purposely provocative.

Photos like these regularly appeared on Cohn's Twitter account during the mid-2010s, and although she posed much less provocatively at the end of the decade and into the 2020s, her style of dress remains less conservative than it was during the 1990s. While it might be convenient to solely attribute this to an overall change in fashion trends over the past few decades, some women in the industry, like

Paula, still prefer the conservative, so-called professional appearance a pantsuit affords. Therefore, the option to dress conservatively has not entirely vanished as notions of what is fashionable have changed.

Cohn's sartorial turn and ensuing mid-2010s self-presentation on Twitter situated her as the quintessential neoliberal woman sportscaster, having checked many postfeminist boxes. She played up her "femininity as a bodily property," doing so in a way that seemed like a conscious, empowered choice. She made herself over to appear younger, through the increased usage of makeup and hair dye, changing her hair color from brown to blonde. Finally, she embraced a turn from a passive sex object to a desiring sexual subject, a turn in which it appears women are actively "up for" sex (Gill 2007), as Cohn appeared to be in the last photo described previously. Observers at *Barstool Sports* (2014) certainly thought Cohn was up for sex in that particular photo—or at least viewed her as a sexual subject and not a sportscaster—when they wrote a tweet that declared that Cohn had been "MILFing EXTRA hard on Sportscenter lately" (emphasis in original). Among my informants, Paula explicitly bemoaned Cohn's turn. "Look at Linda Cohn, how she dresses now," Paula said, in response to a general question about sportscaster attire. "She used to dress in pantsuits, and now they got her in hoochie-mama dresses all the time. And she's old. It's just ridiculous." Paula's continued usage of the word "they" when discussing Cohn is noteworthy. As stated previously, "they" could be Cohn's superiors at ESPN or an ambiguous "they" that includes those who are complicit in the normalization of the gendered appearance double standard. Based on Teitell's (2017) *Globe* article, we might assume either Cohn was told to dress like this by her superiors or she decided to present herself in this manner to stay relevant among her peers. The latter assumption could be valid given her age, a rarity for women in this industry.

Although the turn toward sexual subjectification—often demonstrated in the twenty-first century by way of T-shirts with suggestive phrases and "duck lip" selfies—might appear to be lighthearted and empowering, this mode of representation and, more specifically, the way it is celebrated, is nevertheless problematic. First, this turn is typically only celebrated when taken by women who, like Cohn, are white, heterosexual, and thin, but who, unlike Cohn, are also rela-

tively young (Gill 2007). Second, the turn toward sexual subjectification is sticky because of the way it is often presented as an act of free
will. Rather, like nightclubification itself, taking on the role of desiring sexual subject is an illusion of choice that is problematic because
it privileges the women who adopt it and marginalizes those who
don't (or can't). Postfeminism's pervasive presentation of sexual subjectification is further troublesome as it contributes to rape culture
by giving heterosexual men the impression that "everyday" women
are actively inviting sex when they present themselves in a similar
manner (Gill 2007), rather than simply existing.

This impression has ramifications for women sportscasters, too,
when they engage male sources. As explored later in this chapter, there
is often a presumption of promiscuity that diminishes the perceived
credibility of successful sportscasters and, as explicated in chapter 3,
is sometimes brought to bear on their interactions with male sources
who may be inclined to seek sexual or romantic favors. Again, gendered neoliberalism ensures that the responsibility for resolving mistreatment that results from the pervasive, highly sexualized (self-)
presentation of women sportscasters is placed on the women themselves and not society's institutions. Women who persevere are therefore seen as "built for" the industry, and those who leave or choose
not to enter are not "cut out" for this work. As a result, not only
does gendered neoliberalism encourage many women sportscasters to objectify themselves, but its emphasis on individual responsibility and empowerment in the face of gendered mistreatment also
implicitly absolves the sportscasting industry of any culpability for
the way society at large objectifies women sportscasters. The status
quo of the gendered appearance double standard—and, at present,
nightclubification—thus remain.

The Consequences of Neoliberal (Self-)Presentation

Suffice it to say, many more doors are open to women sportscasters
who accept a neoliberal mode of self-presentation. Women are often
presented with more opportunities when they embrace what makes
them "naturally" different from their men counterparts and therefore place a greater emphasis on their appearance than they do on
their skills. My informants most often referenced FOX Sports side-

line reporter Erin Andrews as an example of a sportscaster whose star quickly rose due to the industry's prioritization of appearance. Specifically, my interview and focus group informants recalled Andrews's well-documented promotion to FOX Sports' top National Football League sideline reporter role in 2014, at the expense of Pam Oliver, an older, widely respected reporter and one of the industry's few sideline reporters of color. Oliver was reassigned to FOX's B crew as a result of Andrews's promotion (Deitsch 2014). For her part, Andrews does not normally wear revealing clothing on the air. In fact, because most of her appearances occur during football season, which takes place during the fall and winter, she is often seen on camera wearing a coat.

Nevertheless, Andrews's status as a sex symbol, one who is not averse to wearing revealing clothing, perhaps comes from her work away from the football field. She has posed numerous times for magazines, including such images as her photo on the cover of a 2017 issue of *Health*, in which she is wearing a red bikini; another photo in the same issue of *Health*, in which she is wearing a highly stylized, white one-piece bathing suit; and a photo in a 2014 issue of *Men's Health* in which she is wearing short denim shorts and a button-down shirt while lying on her side, hair down, painting one of the yard numbers on a football field. Andrews has also been a cohost on *Dancing with the Stars* since the show's eighteenth season in 2014. Throughout her tenure on the show, Andrews has worn many stylish yet revealing dresses, aside from the one that drew Elisabeth Hasselbeck's scrutiny when Andrews was a contestant in 2010. For season 22's finale in 2016, Andrews wore one dress that was so revealing that her stylist, Alyssa Greene, said Andrews needed approval—presumably from the show's producers—before it could be worn on air (Alindogan 2016). "In the end we had to cover up a little more than we would have liked but we still totally went for the sheer sexy look," Greene said (para. 3). These examples are out of the context of Andrews's primary job as a sideline reporter; in particular, the *Health* photos were meant to promote confidence in one's body in light of the news that Andrews had withheld a cervical cancer diagnosis from the public. Nevertheless, these examples can be viewed as being related to her role as a woman sportscaster, insofar as her career as a sports reporter are what made her famous in the first place.

Men in the industry perform the same general function as women, to deliver sports information and commentary. However, as is the case in other industries, it seems it is women sportscasters who need to show their bodies to make a name for themselves. As Sarah Spain stated, men "are allowed to just report." With apologies to *Bleacher Report* and Instagram star Taylor Rooks, no woman sportscaster has used her appearance to make a greater name for herself than Erin Andrews. Given her long-standing willingness to show her body—and the plentiful opportunities afforded to her to do so—it becomes easy to see how her attractiveness is perceived as having been prioritized over her and others' perceived abilities. "I think that Erin got that role [on FOX's top NFL broadcast crew] because she's younger and she's prettier," Lizzy said. "And not to say Erin isn't good at her job—I think she is. But I think she was given that role despite the fact that she wasn't better than [Oliver]." Ken, another undergraduate, had this to say about the Andrews/Oliver situation: "With Erin Andrews, she's more of the eye candy, where she—if you sat in a room with her and Pam Oliver, I think Pam Oliver would know a lot more about football than [Andrews] would know. But it's—they want the prettier girl."

Left unsaid is the extent to which race and age might play a role in Andrews's and Oliver's perceived attractiveness, ability, and credibility. Could it be that Andrews was considered by my informants to be prettier than Oliver because Andrews is white and younger? After all, Anglocentric white femininity, society's idealized notion of beauty and the foundation of the industry's appearance double standard, favors women who are white and have long, blonde hair, like Andrews. Conversely, could it also be that Oliver is deemed to be more knowledgeable about football because Andrews is younger and has blonde hair? The upshot of the prioritization of appearance for women sportscasters is the assumption among sports media consumers—*and* some women sportscasters—that some of the industry's women primarily gain entry or upward mobility in the field because of their appearance. Although attractiveness and journalistic ability are both socially constructed, the perception that a highly attractive sportscaster might have been promoted primarily because of her appearance loosely resembles the findings of the Davis and Krawczyk study

(2010), which suggests that a woman sportscaster's perceived credibility decreases if she is perceived to be significantly more attractive than her peers.

The Appearance Double Standard

While it is clear that a double standard of appearance exists, and that it has been reinforced in the early twenty-first century by gendered neoliberalism, what is not as clear is *why* it exists. Michel Foucault's work on power/knowledge and discourse provides a lens through which we can understand how this double standard came to be and who is (or, better yet, is *not*) responsible for its establishment in sportscasting. If we can recognize that the appearance double standard has been constructed in sportscasting so as to become "common sense," we can further understand how it is maintained by gendered neoliberalism.

Conventional thinking suggests the expectations of appearance placed on women sportscasters—informed by socially embedded notions of white femininity—serve the sexual tastes of what is assumed to be a mostly heterosexual male sports media consumer base. David Portnoy's comment that "we want to see [Sam Ponder] sex it up and be slutty" (Kerr-Dineen 2017, para. 7) embodies this line of thinking. Eddie, a nontraditional-aged undergraduate, offered a similar take during one of my focus groups: "As I said, I mean, look at sports. I'm going to throw out a figure. Probably about 80 percent of [sports media consumers] are men. Supply and demand. What does your audience want to see? . . . I mean, look at the PGA Tour, professional golf. Men are not allowed to wear shorts because, let's face it, guys who are watching it don't want to see men's legs. The LPGA, everyone's wearing skirts. Why? Because the guys want to see the women in skirts."

The perception that it is necessary to prioritize women sportscaster appearance to draw in male consumers presupposes many things. Among other notions, and as I explore in greater detail in the next chapter, this perception assumes that many sports media consumers, heterosexual men or otherwise, don't consume sports media regardless of who is on screen and what they look like. In that same vein, as reported by the *Boston Globe*, Andrea Kremer, a longtime sports television reporter, agreed that the "give men what they want" argument is a dubious one. In her view, the justification for the appearance double standard might be a cover for heterosexual male managers who want to fulfill their own fantasies. "Until we have women in the position to hire," she told the *Globe*, "you will get men who want to hire women they couldn't get dates with in high school" (Teitell 2017, para. 26). Given the #MeToo movement and the many high-profile sexual misconduct allegations within the entertainment (Harvey Weinstein), news (Matt Lauer), sports media (ESPN and NFL Network), and political industries (many men on both sides of the U.S. political spectrum), Kremer's theory seems valid. Following Eddie's and Kremer's logic, the simplest explanation for the appearance double standard, then, is that it serves to titillate male sports media consumers and managers.

Discursively, however, the appearance double standard is more complex than that. Based on what we know about the Foucauldian concept of power, it is fluid and not exercised centrally. The appearance double standard is therefore better understood not solely as an act of power by heterosexual men against women but as a practice that both informs and is informed by what we "know" about the female sportscaster. The experiences and observations shared by my informants, as well as other statements made in mediated texts, indicate that men, women, media consumers, and media managers understand women sportscasters to be hired more for their looks than for their knowledge and skills. This is a practice that has long been visible in sports media—going back to at least CBS's hiring of Phyllis George in 1975—yet, to the best of my knowledge, has not been explicitly declared by any one industry decision maker or documented by any particular sports media organization as standard operating procedure. As a result of the long-standing, implicit priority placed on appearance, most women entering the industry necessarily comply with the appearance double standard. As contemporary standards for what is stylistically acceptable (and expected) have changed, many women in the sportscasting industry now feel as though they must wear revealing clothing, even if they are not asked to do so by their superiors. Women who comply with the double standard and participate in nightclubification therefore risk diminishing their perceived credibility, much in the same way Erin Andrews's qualifications have been called into question.

This process, in which women sportscasters lose perceived credibility as the result of the industry's implicit and explicit emphasis on appearance, exemplifies the Foucauldian concept of power and its lack of a possessor. To the best of my knowledge, men have not held meetings in which they elected to force women in the sports media industry into complying with the appearance double standard or into wearing revealing clothing specifically for the purpose of weakening their credibility. And yet, despite the improbability of such a meeting taking place and as a result of this double standard, women sportscasters must work harder than men to prove that they are qualified. The sportscasting industry—as an amorphous, decentralized entity—established the appearance double standards through consistent, visible hiring and representational practices, not explicit edicts. Similarly, gendered neoliberalism has reinforced and is reinforced by the industry's (in)actions with respect to the appearance double standard. Because the gendered appearance double standard has diminished women sportscasters' authority to some extent, women in the industry must also endure a double standard of credibility.

Credibility Double Standard

As I argue throughout this volume, the sportscasting industry's gendered appearance double standard serves as the foundation for nearly all gendered obstacles women sportscasters endure—certainly those examined in this book. Each of these obstacles inform and reinforce the others. Thus, I turn now to the industry's gendered credibility double standard, which assumes women sportscasters to be inferior to their male peers with respect to both skill and knowledge. This credibility double standard both informs and is informed by the notion that women in the industry are hired primarily because of their looks. It is also buttressed by idealized notions of white feminine comportment (Deliovsky 2010), whereas the ideal female sportscaster would be too nurturing, too deferential to men, and too concerned with her own appearance to be as skilled and knowledgeable as her male peers. Most importantly, an ideal white feminine demeanor also dictates that women would not offer sports-related opinions, especially those that criticize our (white, heteronormative) patriarchy. In sum, the gendered credibility double standard is yet another obstacle legitimized by gendered neoliberalism, to the extent that the ideal neoliberal female sportscaster subject deftly navigates the double standard with little to no institutional support while those who are not ideal—those who "can't hack it"—do not.

Although it helps both men and women sportscasters to be perceived as credible, the standard of presumed credibility—or the extent to which a person is perceived to be a skilled and knowledgeable source of sports knowledge—is inconsistently applied to men and women in the industry. A man sportscaster's qualifications are taken for granted by members of the sports media, media consumers, athletes, and coaches more often than those of a woman sportscaster. This credibility double standard is manifest in an assumption of woman sportscaster promiscuity, in gendered skepticism of a woman sportscaster's abilities and knowledge, and in the responses to woman sportscaster opinions. Collectively, these manifestations demonstrate the negative impact the appearance double standard has on the female sportscaster's perceived credibility.

The Promiscuous Female Sportscaster

Among the many manifestations of the credibility double standard is the presumption that some women who have entered (and are ascending in) the industry have performed sexual favors for their male superiors and sources in exchange for preferential treatment and exclusive access. One of my informants, Lizzy, has heard her colleagues suggest she slept with managers as well as athletes to gain favor. In a profile of multiple women sportscasters published in the *Hollywood Reporter* ("10 All-Star Female Reporters" 2013), Rachel Nichols, host of ESPN's *The Jump*, provides support for Lizzy's insights, stating that the assumption of sexual quid pro quo is often just the result of a woman in sports media doing her job well. "And when a female sports journalist gets a great story," Nichols says, "you can almost set your watch by how quickly whispers start that she must have slept with the player to get it" (para. 1). Similarly, in an article published by the *Seattle Times*, Sarah Spain stated that, within her first two weeks in a new position at a startup sports website, "a longtime beat reporter told a team public relations representative [that Spain] must be sleeping with a player because she was getting better stories than other reporters" (Kaminski 2014, para. 3). Lizzy believes male sportscasters are not accused of sleeping with their managers and sources because those managers and sources are typically men. Within the context of women superiors and sources, Lizzy added, "Can you imagine a man being told that? He gets to cover the WNBA and, 'Oh, it's because he's sleeping with the women.' That doesn't happen. That's a completely ridiculous double standard."

Lizzy's comments shine a light on sportscasting's reliance on white feminine ideals of conduct, insofar as it is assumed that a woman could only have achieved upward mobility by serving men. Her comments also expose sports and sportscasting's heterosexism. The underlying assumptions at play within her experience and observation— aside from the perception that she is not qualified for her job—are that a male sportscaster would not sleep with another man to gain favor and that men in the industry do not need to perform sexual favors with women because women generally are not in a position to ask for them. As was the case with the appearance double standard there was (to my knowledge) no committee of men in the industry that ceremoniously chose to perpetuate an assumption that successful (and, especially, youthful and attractive) women in the industry have slept their way into their roles. Instead, this assumption is in large part the consequence of the appearance double standard, bolstered by the normalization of white feminine beauty and behavior.

Gendered Skepticism

Another manifestation of the credibility double standard is the skepticism women sportscasters receive from media consumers and sources regarding their credentials and sports knowledge, often in the form of sports knowledge quizzes. Jane reported attending events in which she would be quizzed on her sports knowledge by random attendees while nearby male colleagues would not face similar scrutiny. "And I was, like, 'You know, you don't have to be a walking trivia person to be a strong sports reporter,'" she said. "And the person standing right next to me does the exact same thing. You didn't ask him who won some championship in a year before he was born." Stephanie, the baseball podcaster, said that, to test her knowledge of the sport, men often ask her if she understands baseball's incredibly complex infield fly rule. The rule is designed to prevent a defensive team from using deception to record two or three outs in one play by intentionally dropping a popup on the infield and throwing out unsuspecting and necessarily stationary baserunners. "Like, really? Really? That's the test? Why? Why the infield fly rule? If I had a dollar for every time I've been asked if I know the infield fly rule, I could pay off the umpire to stop enforcing the infield fly rule."

Similarly, Patricia has often received emails from her viewers attempting to stump her and question her editorial choices, while Paula stated that a woman sportscaster spends her first year on the job just proving her credibility. Women sportscasters especially spend time proving themselves if they are covering a sport like American football, which does not have a major women's professional equivalent, aside from the relatively obscure Legends Football League, formerly known as the Lingerie Football League. "You look at me as a woman and say, 'Well, she's a woman. What the hell does she know?'" Paula said. "You're already judged—that's already the first impression that they get. So, you have to prove yourself."

Sometimes this gendered skepticism comes into play when women sportscasters cover a press conference or access a locker room. According to both Patricia and Marie, security guards often question their ability to access those spaces, despite the fact they wear press credentials around their necks and carry around video equipment. Patricia said, "We have big cameras and tripods, but [security and team personnel] feel the need to stop us and ask us, 'Do you guys know where you're going? Are you supposed to be here? Do you know what you're doing?' No, we just carry around these cameras for fun." During the 2015 NFL season, an usher denied two women print journalists entry into the Jacksonville Jaguars' locker room at Lucas Oil Stadium in Indianapolis ("Female Sports Writers Denied" 2015). Graham Watson (2015a, 2015b), one of the two reporters, ironically tweeted that the usher "apparently [was] not aware that women cover sports" and added, "I have covered male sporting events all over the world and it took coming to Indianapolis to face my first gender discrimination." Coincidentally, Watson and her colleague were attending the game as part of the Associated Press Sports Editors' Diversity Weekend ("Female Sports Writers Denied" 2015).

In addition, male athletes and coaches sometimes openly express their doubts about women in sports media and the knowledge they possess. Then–Carolina Panthers quarterback Cam Newton laughed when Jordan Rodrigue, a print journalist with the *Charlotte Observer*, asked him about the receiving routes one of his teammates had been running in recent games. Newton chuckled and said, "It's funny to hear a female talk about routes" (Hull et al 2019). In *Hollywood Reporter's* "10 All-Star Female Reporters" (2013), NBC *Sunday Night Football* sideline reporter Michele Tafoya told the story of a time, early in her career, when she met Bobby Knight, one of the all-time winningest (and surliest) coaches in college basketball, for an interview. Just before the interview, Knight asked Tafoya if she was "any good at this" (para. 9). When Tafoya told him that she *was* good and that she felt she had been assigned to interview him for a reason, Knight replied, "Because, you know there are a lot of women who do this who stink at it." Knight dropped his skepticism after they both agreed that there are also a lot of men who are not very good at it. Tafoya evidently had proved her mettle to a man who literally questioned her qualifications, and perhaps expected her to make mistakes, simply because she was a woman. Knight has never been known to be friendly; thus he could have just as easily expressed skepticism toward a neophyte man sportscaster. Nevertheless, given his qualifying comments, Knight used Tafoya's gender to justify his query about her credentials.

Men are not the only ones who express gendered skepticism. In one of my focus groups, two undergraduate women stated that they preferred listening to male sportscasters because, in general, they believed men to be more well informed. One of those two women, Cindy, even said that she would be initially skeptical of a woman sportscaster talking about a men's sport like American football. As is the case with presumed woman sportscaster promiscuity, these comments are based on a presumption of male sportscasters possessing superior knowledge that is largely informed by the appearance double standard and white feminine ideals. That is, because it is assumed that women sportscasters are hired for their looks and that their appearance is their primary concern, women in the industry cannot possibly be as skilled and knowledgeable as their male colleagues.

Ability to Give Opinions

The determination of who possesses the authority to give their opinions in sports debates is informed by gendered skepticism and white feminine notions of subservience and deference to men. As a result, women are more likely to be belittled or dehumanized for offering their sports opinions than their male peers. Many of the women sportscasters I spoke with, as well as my focus group informants, have either experienced or observed this manifestation of the credibility double standard.

Marie told me she receives many more emails than her male boss (who also appears on air) when she and her boss share their opinions on television. "I just think a lot of times people are very harsh, very, very harsh in terms of a sports opinion," she said. Her opinion "can be different than my boss's, which is fine in sports, but he won't get an email. I will." Patricia, who also cohosts a podcast with a male colleague, stated that while she does receive negative feedback online for her opinions on the podcast—along the lines of "that girl's an idiot"—her colleague has never received negative feedback. "And," Patricia said, "we've actually experimented where we've tried to—he will purposely say the same thing that I say. Either just word it a little bit differently, or after a few minutes expire, he will say almost word for word what I say. And, always, if there's any [negative] comments, it's directed towards me—not towards [him]."

The past decade and a half has seen an increase in the number of (mostly male) sports television talk-show hosts who tend to speak loudly and bloviate. Present-day sports media personalities such as Stephen A. Smith, Skip Bayless, Tony Kornheiser, and Colin Cowherd come to mind. These hosts, and the manner in which they speak—loudly and often over their cohosts—exemplify the impunity with which men are permitted to give their sports opinions. Women, with few exceptions and as explained in chapter 2, are not given similar platforms on which they can share their opinions. Those who do have the latitude to give their opinions face harsher criticism than their male counterparts. The strident gendered criticism women sportscasters often face can disincentivize women from sharing their opinions, which can result in the perceptions that women do not have opinions, are ill informed, or are on the air simply to moderate the debate and capture the attention of heterosexual male viewers.

My focus group informants cited the men mentioned previously, as well as Philadelphia sports media personality and antagonist Howard Eskin, as examples of men who freely state their often abrasive opinions. Marcus said this about the aforementioned men: A man like that is "just a loudmouth who doesn't really say a lot of stuff. Right? Doesn't know what they're talking about. They are an opinion piece, really, to kind of stir the pot, if you will. I don't think—I think people are more accepting of a guy doing that than they are of a girl doing that."

When I asked members of another focus group if they could envision a woman as an opinionated sports media antagonist, one informant shook her head and said that such a woman would be called "a bitch with a capital B." Lisa, another informant in the same focus group, believed that such a woman sportscaster might be permitted on the air but would quickly be removed, stating: "I don't know how long she would be allowed to remain on the air, if she were to be that confrontational. I think it's more acceptable in a man, even if it causes scandal. But, I feel like in a woman, they would milk it for whatever attention it might bring, but then, she'd be gone." Another informant from that focus group, Lenny, offered Nanci Donnellan—known in the 1990s as the Fabulous Sports Babe—as an example of a woman who enjoyed a relatively short time in the limelight while providing inflammatory sports opinions. Donnellan hosted a syndicated sports talk radio show for ESPN Radio that was also simulcast on ESPN2. "She had that kind of approach that you're talking about—real aggressive, real 'in your face.' And she was real big for a while, but that disappeared fast." Indeed, *The Fabulous Sports Babe* lasted only three years on the ESPN family of networks.

In instances in which women sportscasters *are* given the latitude to share their opinions, sometimes the backlash from sports media consumers still serves to silence the sportscaster. Julie DiCaro (2015), then a sports talk radio personality in Chicago, wrote about the backlash she received for sharing her opinions in the wake of rape allegations made against National Hockey League player Patrick Kane. DiCaro, who has been vocal about her experience as a victim of rape, received rape and death threats on Twitter as a result of her opinions on the Kane case. To her, online interactions such as these make it clear that "you may not share your sports opinion while, at the same time, being a woman" (para. 2). These online interactions became the basis of the "#MoreThanMean" public service announcement, which demonstrated that gendered sports media consumer backlash against female sportscaster opinions is especially strong on social media.

That backlash is even stronger when women sportscasters of color express their opinions. In the fall of 2017, Jemele Hill, then an anchor for ESPN's *SportsCenter*, twice drew the ire of sports media consumers when she took to social media to call U.S. president Donald Trump a "white supremacist" and to encourage a boycott of the Dallas Cowboys over its national anthem policies in the wake of the NFL's police brutality protests, led by Colin Kaepernick (Harrison et al. 2019). Unintentionally or not, Hill, who resigned from ESPN in 2018, regularly flouted the white feminine ideals governing women sportscasters. Not only did she often express opinions that questioned white patriarchal policies and institutions, but she was also a Black woman sportscaster who frequently wore her hair in braids and therefore did not conform to the Anglocentric ideals of feminine beauty. Though she never explicitly admitted that the white feminine, neoliberal expectations placed on women sportscasters were too much for her to bear, it is easy to imagine them playing at least a small role in her decision to leave television. A glance at the responses she often garnered on social media (Harrison et al. 2020) suggests that the consistency with which she defied white feminine ideals certainly played a role in her status as a controversial figure among sports media consumers. It is also not surprising that when Jason Whitlock (2020) warned Maria Taylor about coming across as too "angry" to sports fans, Whitlock cited Hill as an example of a sportscaster whose career in television ended because she did not display a happy (white feminine) temperament. As gendered neoliberalism normalizes the white femininity Hill consistently disrupted, we can conclude that gendered neoliberalism serves white supremacy as well as patriarchy. Many scholars have argued that, in Western cultures especially, patriarchy and white supremacy are one and the same. Such is the reality for women working in sportscasting.

Conclusion

It has been well known that, not unlike women in other industries, women sportscasters must navigate gendered double standards of appearance and credibility. Nevertheless, it is worth examining just how these double standards are constructed by (and contribute to) gendered neoliberal discourse that is the foundation of the idealized female sportscaster subject. In sum, gendered neoliberalism not only reinforces the two double standards analyzed in this chapter but, in normalizing Anglocentric femininity, does so while serving white supremacy. If a woman of color is a skilled, knowledgeable reporter but cannot get on the air without lengthening and straightening her short or braided hair—a distinct possibility—that's racism as much as it is sexism. The appearance and credibility double standards are therefore simultaneously gendered and racialized.

The appearance double standard—a deeply rooted, systemic practice—diminishes the perceived credibility of women sportscasters in a way that has allowed both double standards to be taken for granted over time. An inequitable standard of acceptable and expected clothing for women is apparent within this contradictory discourse. Just as extant scholarship suggests women sportscasters can look "too sexy" to be credible, women sportscasters can also *dress* too sexy to be deemed by some as credible or even decent for television. However, the clothing that is deemed too sexy for some consumers is becoming increasingly expected in broadcast television newsrooms and studios. This paradox forces women sportscasters to choose between two generally undesirable options: they can either dress too sexy to be deemed credible or decent, or they can risk not advancing in a career they have spent time and money training for. The illusion of choice coupled with the paradoxical clothing paradigm women sportscasters must navigate are postfeminist—and therefore neoliberal—phenomena, insofar as discourses of agency and an entanglement or contradiction of feminist and antifeminist discourses are at the heart of those phenomena.

Discourses of agency and empowerment are disingenuous and problematic within the context of sportscasting; they almost always call on women to self-regulate their bodies and appearance (Gill and

Scharff 2011) and do so in a way that conforms with idealized Anglo-centric femininity. Additionally, if women sportscasters were truly empowered to dress or look how they wanted, they could do so without being told they looked too sexy or not sexy enough. The entanglement of feminist and antifeminist discourses is also problematic because either can be co-opted to advance an idea or structure of domination. In the case of women sportscasters, accusations that some wear clothing that is unnecessarily revealing (a feminist discourse) can be co-opted as evidence that most women in the industry are hired to be "eye candy" (an antifeminist discourse).

The entanglement of such discourses has therefore served to diminish women sportscaster credibility, leading to assumptions that some upwardly mobile women sportscasters are devoid of legitimate journalistic skills and have performed sexual favors on their way toward achieving success. As I argue in the next chapter, the assumptions associated with the gendered credibility double standard have made it challenging for women to obtain certain roles (such as play-by-play announcing) in the sportscasting industry. Since gendered neoliberalism dictates who the ideal female sportscaster is, the onus for making women more visible in those roles is discursively placed on the women who aspire to them. As a result, when women sportscasters obtain these roles—and also when they fail to do so—gendered neoliberalism serves its purpose, legitimizing the practices (double standards, bias in hiring and development) that contribute to the absence of women in those roles.

TWO

Sportscasting's Glass Booth

On August 24, 2015, former U.S. Olympic softball player Jessica Mendoza made her debut as an analyst for ESPN's coverage of Major League Baseball. In doing so, she became the first woman in the network's history to provide baseball commentary from inside the sportscasting booth. Six days later, Mendoza, who had previously been assigned to ESPN's *Baseball Tonight* studio show, as well as the network's coverage of the NCAA Women's and Men's College World Series, was introduced to a larger audience when she filled in for the suspended Curt Schilling as an analyst on ESPN's *Sunday Night Baseball*. In October of that same year, Mendoza stood alongside play-by-play commentator Dan Shulman and fellow analyst John Kruk as she became the first woman commentator ever assigned to a televised Major League Baseball postseason game. After that game, Mendoza's presence in the booth garnered a highly publicized wave of gendered criticism, led by Atlanta-area sports talk radio host Mike Bell, who tweeted, "Yes tell us Tits McGhee when you're up there hitting the softball [do] you see many 95 mile an hour [fastballs]?" (Hill 2015).[1]

After the 2015 MLB postseason, Mendoza permanently replaced Schilling on the *Sunday Night Baseball* announcing team. Kruk was replaced by Aaron Boone, who two years later became manager of the New York Yankees. Shulman would also leave the announcing crew after the 2017 season to spend more time with his family. Having outlasted her first three fellow *Sunday Night Baseball* commentators, Mendoza found herself in a position rarely achieved by women in sportscasting, especially those assigned to cover a men's sport: ESPN built a team of announcers around her, adding Matt Vasgersian (play-by-play) and Alex Rodriguez (color commentary) to the booth before the 2018 season.

Mendoza is neither the first nor the last woman to step into the sportscasting booth and provide commentary for a men's sport. In 1987 Gayle Sierens became the first woman play-by-play announcer for a televised National Football League game, and in 2001 Lesley Visser was the first woman to serve as a color commentator for an NFL game ("Westwood One/CBS Sports" 2001). Beth Mowins became the first woman play-by-play announcer for a *nationally televised* NFL game in 2017 (DiCaro 2017), and in the same year, Doris Burke, Kara Lawson, and Sarah Kustok were all given full-time NBA game analyst opportunities by various organizations (Spanberg 2018). Lastly, Hannah Storm and Andrea Kremer led the first all-woman sportscast for an NFL game in 2018, albeit on an alternate audio stream for Amazon Prime's sportscast of *Thursday Night Football*. Although there have been women who have blazed trails into the booth both before and after Jessica Mendoza, I start this chapter with her story because her introduction to ESPN's baseball audience—and the response it garnered—brought sportscasting's inequitable representation of women back into public discussion, with a specific eye toward the roles to which men and women in the industry are typically assigned. While the industry has been slow to integrate women into the sportscasting booth, there are roles—such as anchor, host, and sideline or field reporter—to which women have been increasingly assigned with little backlash.

As with the appearance and credibility double standards, gendered neoliberalism serves to reinforce this status quo too. While women have historically been excluded from certain roles, with a few recent exceptions like Mendoza and Mowins, the industry has not been proactive in rectifying the invisibility of women in the sportscasting booth, especially for high-profile men's sports. Instead, I argue that, just as gendered neoliberalism calls on women to be entrepreneurial in how they navigate sportscasting's gendered and racialized double standards, these women are also left to their own devices as they pursue such sportscasting roles. Based on the insights provided to me by my informants, women have had difficulty integrating the sportscasting booth because, among other reasons, the credibility double standard affords them a lack of opportunities to hone the type of skills that are needed to succeed as commentators. Additionally, the lack of such opportunities also precludes many women from even developing a passion for such roles. As a result, sportscasting educators, managers, and colleagues often assume that women either cannot or do not want to develop play-by-play skills.

I further argue this assumption is informed discursively, in a Foucauldian sense, not only by the credibility double standard but also by the historic lack of visibility of women in such positions. As the saying goes, "You can't be what you can't see." However, while media organizations regularly trade in an economy of visibility in the era of popular feminism (Banet-Weiser 2018), whereby simply placing a woman in the booth is considered progress, the publicity garnered from giving women like Mowins, Mendoza, and Burke a headset does not change the structures that generally preclude women from pursuing commentary roles. We can simultaneously applaud ESPN for putting these women on the air while also recalling that, as related in chapter 1, Burke was mandated to see a wardrobe consultant before being given NBA television assignments. Postfeminist discourse also plays a factor, to the extent that its reassertion of sexual difference (Gill 2007) would have us believe that women lack a natural inclination toward play-by-play. After all, in my experience as a sports media educator, many more women than men confirm they have never had any desire to be live event commentators, while for many more aspiring men sportscasters, play-by-play is the ultimate job aspiration. Thus, through discourse informed by popular feminism and postfeminism, gendered neoliberalism reinforces the status quo. Instead of acknowledging sportscasting's historical exclusion of women as pivotal to their lack of integration into these roles, gendered neoliberalism gives the industry a pass. The onus is therefore on women to develop and demonstrate more of a willingness and a stubborn desire to enter the booth than their men counterparts. The reality of this inequity ignores the discursive and material obstacles that present themselves to women and girls, often before they even aspire to become sportscasters. It should be acknowledged that seeing women like Mendoza and Burke in the booth and courtside, respectively, for high-profile men's sports can have a positive impact on young women and girls. Conversely, the backlash to women entering the booth can have the reverse impact, informing and being informed by the status quo.

The constructed deficiencies I describe are with respect to the play-by-play announcing and color commentary (or analyst) positions for high-profile men's sports, sportscasting's most coveted and prestigious roles. For women sportscasters, these roles are also the most elusive in the industry, so much so that they appear to be contained within what I call a *glass booth*. My usage of this phrase is derived from the *glass ceiling*, a metaphorical barrier to upward mobility that makes it possible for women to see the top of their respective industries yet makes actually reaching the top difficult to achieve. Likewise, through their work with sports media organizations, women sportscasters have as close a view of the work that takes place in the sportscasting booth as anyone, but few of the women who want to be play-by-play announcers and color analysts find themselves in those roles for men's sports. Later in this chapter, I explicate the various reasons these positions are usually not given to women.

I frame my analysis in this chapter according to sports media's gendered hierarchy. As Pam Creedon (1998) and others have written, those working within the sports media industry are not unaffected by the marginalization of women's sports. According to Creedon, men's sports are hegemonically positioned as *the* destination for successful journalists and media personalities, while women's sports are constructed as a space that ambitious journalists want to avoid. That is, as a result of its taken-for-granted prominence and priority within the sports media complex, aspiring sports journalists more often pursue careers covering men's sports. This distinction between men's and women's sports is important because, if men's and women's sports were given equal treatment (Musto, Cooky, and Messner 2016) and equal airtime (Cooky, Messner, and Musto 2014) by sportscasting organizations, and were thus viewed equally by sports media personalities and consumers, the approach I take in this chapter would necessarily be different.

Consider the career arcs of many of the women I mentioned. Why was Jessica Mendoza, a former softball Olympian, not satisfied with analyzing Women's College World Series games? Before calling NFL games (and college football games before that), Beth Mowins handled play-by-play duties during ESPN's coverage of collegiate women's basketball, women's volleyball, and softball—plenty of work for a sportscaster. Doris Burke and Kara Lawson both covered collegiate and professional women's basketball in various capacities. Why take their talents to the NBA? As Lesley Visser once stated, "Women who get into sports journalism don't want to cover women's sports. They want to cover sports that lead to success" (Cramer 1994, 169). The implication, however overstated it may be, is that men's sports are viewed—even among many women in sports media—as the pinnacle of sportscasting and sports print journalism assignments, in large part because there is greater money and perceived prestige to be earned by covering men's sports. As a result of the disparity in the quality and quantity of coverage between men's and women's sports, the former currently holds larger audiences, and therefore larger ad revenues while women's sports are marginalized and "symbolically annihilated" (Cooky, Messner, and Musto 2015; Tuchman 1979). Men's sports are therefore taken for granted as superior and more prestigious than women's sports. Thus, this chapter is not a discussion of the paucity of women sportscasters in certain roles overall, given the accepted prevalence of women in women's sports coverage. Instead, this chapter discusses the (in)visibility of women sportscasters in certain roles in coverage of men's sports.

I begin my analysis of the gendered neoliberal construction of sportscasting's glass booth by analyzing the discourse that constructs the sportscasting role for which women are often perceived to be ideally suited: the sideline or field reporter position. Although women are equally visible in the sports television anchor chair, especially at the national level, I devote particular attention to the sideline or field reporter role as it is the position within sportscasting that is the most gendered and also the most disputed, among consumers and professionals alike, in terms of its utility. In its origins, the position was meant to serve as a moderator of sorts for a non-serious, irrelevant sideshow to the actual sporting event. This purpose, in addition to the prioritization of appearance that has coincided with the proliferation of women hired into that role over the past five decades, has contributed to the construction of women sideline reporters as, according to one informant, "cheerleaders with microphones." Later, I examine the roles contained within sportscasting's glass booth, play-by-play announcer and color commentator. I analyze the various (often gendered neoliberal) arguments—those made by my informants as well as those found within mass mediated texts—for why so few women are assigned to these positions.

Like many of the other phenomena analyzed throughout the remainder of this book, sportscasting's glass booth has a mutually informing relationship with the industry's gendered and racialized appearance and credibility double standards. In this case, because of the prioritization of appearance for women, they are not viewed as credible or knowledgeable sources of sports information capable of articulating what is happening on the field, the court, or the rink for sports media consumers. Thus, women sportscasters have rarely broken the glass barrier built around the sportscasting booth. Even though the reasons for a lack of women play-by-play announcers and analysts for men's sports are numerous and complex, gendered neoliberalism places the responsibility for their invisibility squarely on their shoulders.

"Cheerleaders with Microphones"

In spite of sportscasting's glass booth, there exists a role within the industry to which women are assigned with relatively little resistance from decision-makers and sports media consumers. In the hierarchy of the sportscasting industry, no on-air position is perceived as ideally suited for women as much as the sideline reporter role. In a video interview for the *Hollywood Reporter* (2015), sports television studio host Michelle Beadle said, "We're not just sideline reporters anymore," implying sideline reporting was theretofore the only role for women in the industry. Historically, the construction of this position has not only confined women to a very narrow set of sportscasting boundaries but has also served to support the gendered neoliberal discourse that serves to keep women on the periphery of the industry's hierarchy. Specifically, the discourse goes, if there is a role earmarked for women, one that they can obtain with little resistance, and if gendered neoliberalism's reassertion of sexual difference tells us that there are certain skills women possess that men do not (and vice versa) then women *would do best to* pursue careers in sideline and field reporting.

Although there have been prominent men sideline reporters, such as the late Craig Sager, Ken Rosenthal, and David Aldridge in recent years, and in spite of the fact that women *are* assigned to other sportscasting roles, when my focus group informants discussed women sportscasters, they almost always referred to women who were sideline or field reporters at the time, such as Erin Andrews, Doris Burke, or Pam Oliver. Further, as I have discovered through speaking with my own women sports media students, others almost always assume they want to be sideline reporters when they express an interest in pursuing a sportscasting career. This assumption is often correct, due in part to the narrow representations of women in sportscasting. That is, many young women *do* aspire to become sideline reporters because it may be easiest for them to imagine themselves in the roles in which they are most represented in the media. Often, though, this assumption that aspiring women sportscasters want to be sideline reporters is incorrect; many of the aspiring women sportscasters I have spoken with want to be play-by-play announcers, analysts, and hosts. Yet, when viewed through a lens of Foucauldian power, the easy assumption exists because, in live sporting event coverage, women are usually only seen or heard from the sidelines. This narrow representation of women in the industry is therefore materially and discursively significant.

The sideline reporter role is also fraught due to its own socially constructed subjectivity. According to one of my focus group informants, Lenny, women sideline reporters are analogous to "cheerleaders with microphones." Implicit and explicit references to cheerleaders can be traced throughout sideline reporter discourse. The comparison to cheerleaders, and the stereotypes associated with them, would suggest that the female sideline reporter is typically a young and attractive yet passive observer who serves to provide emotional support for male athletes and colleagues. Perhaps not coincidentally, the utility of the sideline reporter role has also long been in dispute among members of the sports media and media consumers, given the relatively small amount of airtime sideline reporters receive and the content they provide when they are on air. During the average football game, for example, a sideline reporter gives a brief report just before kickoff and just after halftime. When time permits, the reporter also interviews players after the contest. If there are no significant injuries during the game, these may be the only times the reporter is seen and heard. Compared to the play-by-play announcer and analyst, who are permitted to speak freely throughout the contest—and are the ones usually heard during the event's most important moments—the sideline reporter is given little opportunity to affect the telecast of a game. The relative invisibility of the sideline reporter is partly why the utility of the role is in dispute and why even the women sportscasters I interviewed have such varied opinions of the position.

Not only did some of my informants struggle to see the utility in the sideline reporter role, many disavowed any aspirations of being assigned to the sidelines. Consider these comments from Marie:

> I fucking hate it. I have blonde hair and I'm tall. I don't look anything like Erin Andrews other than the fact that we have blonde hair, we're both tall, and we both have faces. People immediately assume "Oh, are you a sideline reporter?" "You must do sideline." "You should apply for a sideline job." I don't want to do it. Personally, I think it's not really essential to a broadcast. I'm glad they have it, but I cannot—I will never be just a sideline reporter because I just don't think that—for me, I want more responsibility other than saying, "This person just left the game. I talked to the trainer. It's an ankle issue. Back to you." No, that's just not me.

As noted previously, most aspiring women sportscasters I have spoken to encounter a recurring assumption that they are aspiring sideline reporters; Marie's experience corroborates this observation. Moreover, it seems that Marie has a disdain for the role because she is immediately thought of by others as a sideline reporter simply because of a superficial resemblance to Erin Andrews, who, aside from Doris Burke, may be the most recognizable woman in sportscasting. Not only does Marie believe the position to be non-essential to a sports broadcast, but she believes the role does not give the person holding it much responsibility.

Lizzy had earned a sideline reporter assignment at one point in her career. She supported Marie's assertions, stating that although she "respected" the position, she thought its utility could be improved if sideline reporters had more opportunities to inject their own insights into a telecast. She explained: "They aren't really allowed to give their opinion or really weigh in on the conversation at all. It's kind of just little moments and brief things. And that kind of limits the role to such a—well, really, not that valuable." Lizzy's "respect" for the position echoed Marie's statement that she was "glad" the sideline reporter position exists. Their quasi-reverence for the role could be read as a sort of compulsory gratitude since the position has long stood as the only role through which women could have a presence in telecasts of primetime men's sporting events. Marie and Lizzy also expressed a deference for the women who have held and currently hold the sideline reporter role but believe the position to possess potential that remains untapped.

Nancy, a sportscasting hall-of-famer who was also one of the first women assigned to the sideline reporter position, is also ambivalent about the role. While she admitted having "mixed feelings" about the position, she adamantly requested that I not downplay its significance because "there are only three people in a broadcast, right?" a reference to the play-by-play announcer, color commentator, and sideline reporter positions. However, she also said that she has challenged aspiring women sportscasters to dream beyond the sideline reporter role: "I know how hard sideline [reporting] is, but play-by-play is really hard. I don't want them to be afraid of it. . . . I feel a little like I've done my job [paving the way for more women to enter the industry]. I've opened up all these things so that the next [generation can] take over the play-by-play."

Patricia had also worked as a sideline reporter at one point in her career. She, too, expressed ambivalence regarding the position. For her, the position was "a lot of fun"; she felt the reporter adds value to a sports telecast because they can offer information and insights that cannot be gleaned by the announcers working in the broadcast booth above the field or by a local television reporter twenty minutes after the conclusion of the game in the locker room. The sideline reporter "is adding value to the broadcast whether you're just taking it for granted or not," she said. Conversely, Patricia also felt that the utility of the position may be in dispute because it is primarily staffed by women. "I think that oftentimes, because it's become a woman's role, people just feel as though it's a throwaway role," she said, before explaining that many sports media consumers often assume sideline reporters are being fed information by another member of the telecast crew and not finding their own information. "It kind of sucks, honestly, because [they're] doing a great job." The assumption that sideline reporters are being fed their insights, or that those insights add little to a broadcast, might be informed at least in part by the appearance double standard—and, by extension, the double standard of credibility—examined in the previous chapter. After all, if women sideline reporters are hired to attract heterosexual male viewers, what do they really know about sports? What do they really know about reporting? When talking about the roles women are permitted to perform in sportscasting, Stephanie said, "We're allowed to be the sideline reporter who's cute and makes sort of stupid observations about things." It is one thing to be perceived as providing inconsequential information, it is yet another thing to be known for that as well as for being hired for your looks. Just as perceived woman sportscaster credibility is diminished by the prioritization of appearance, so is her perceived ability to be an autonomous journalist capable of finding and reporting relevant information she may or may not have gathered herself.

Lenny's "cheerleaders with microphones" analogy during his focus group discussion was precipitated by a similar appraisal of women sideline reporters by another participant. These comments, made by a middle-aged woman, Teresa, emphasize the "emotional support" a cheerleader-like figure might provide: "And, I think, too, that somehow, either perceived, or for real, the men seem to do the more serious stuff. For example, [for my favorite baseball team,] you would hear men break down a pitching sequence but you would hear [the woman field reporter ask], 'How did it feel to hit that homerun?' And, the women—whether it's intended or not—they cover more the emotional, human side. The men cover a little more of the intellectual, really hardcore sports side."

The constructed image of the sideline reporter as an emotionally supportive cheerleader with a microphone has been discursively constructed through verbal and written texts, images, and, as told by Teresa, highly visible practices. Since appearance often takes precedence over ability in the hiring of women sportscasters, and because of the information the sideline reporter gathers, women in the industry (especially sideline reporters) are often viewed as serving as both "eye candy" and emotional support. Idealized notions of white femininity, as explored in chapter 1, also play a role in the reporter as cheerleader construct. Not only does white femininity (Deliovsky 2010) dictate that the ideal feminine woman should resemble a stereotypical cheerleader—thin and youthful with long, preferably blonde hair—but she should also behave as such, always happy and concerned with her appearance.

The construct of a cheerleader with a microphone is not newly formed. It has been constructed over time, with its origins dating back to the 1970s. The sideline reporter role was originally conceived as a non-serious foil to the buttoned-up business that took place between the commentators in the broadcast booth. The first person assigned to that role was a man, Jim Lampley, now a veteran sportscaster who, over the course of his career, has primarily covered the Olympics and boxing. In an article written by Tommy Crags (2009, para. 2) for *Deadspin*, Lampley acknowledged that he was hired by ABC Sports in 1974 as a recent college graduate after what he described as a months-long, "gimmicky" search for a new, young reporter who could serve as part of the network's college football commentary team and "represent the face and voice of the American college student." Lampley admitted the content he delivered in the 1970s was not overly relevant to the games being played on the football field. "I never thought for a second that what we did was vital," Lampley said. "What had been envisioned was that, several times during the telecast, they'd throw to the sideline, where a college-aged reporter would do something, within 24 seconds, on Herbie the mascot buffalo or the cheerleader who won homecoming queen or whatever" (para. 14). When Lampley asked to be removed from the sideline reporter role for, as he said, the sake of his "dignity," he was replaced by Anne Simon, who Lampley described as a "beautiful young woman" (para. 16).

Lampley's analysis of the sideline reporter position after Simon succeeded him is relevant to the construct of the female sideline reporter subject. Not only did he posit that most sideline reporters are women who are "bright, eager to become *legitimate* sports reporters" (para.

16, emphasis mine), he also argued that women are placed in what he called "an awkward position" (para. 16) due to the relatively light-hearted approach the position has always called for. In Lampley's view, when women sideline reporters give information that is not particularly relevant, it is easy for sports media consumers to conclude that the reporter was hired to serve as eye candy, especially since he believes producers have strategically hired attractive women to, theoretically, draw larger heterosexual male audiences. Lampley believes this strategy to be dubious, stating, "Obviously, they think [women sideline reporter appearance] filters into the mix that prompts more people to stay and watch a telecast. I just doubt that's the case. If my goal today was to look at a beautiful woman, I don't have to turn on the Notre Dame–USC telecast. I've got 147 channels to choose from" (para. 16).

Lampley's observations suggest the purposeful prioritization of appearance for women sportscasters perpetuates the perception among sports media consumers that female sideline reporters are hired for their looks. This conclusion is a byproduct of both the double standard of appearance and the initial conceptualization (and continued utilization) of the sideline reporter role.

The "cheerleaders with microphones" analogy has also been constructed in a similar fashion. The same *Deadspin* article profiling Lampley also described former *Monday Night Football* sideline reporter Lisa Guerrero, a former actress and NFL cheerleader, as "a natural step in the evolution of a position that was defiantly stupid from its very conception. . . . More than anyone . . . Guerrero was exactly what the job had called for, from the first: a smiling, pleasantly daft *cheerleader*" (para. 12, emphasis mine).

For their part, my focus group informants also exhibited an ambivalent attitude toward the sideline reporter role. One informant, Phil, said that the halftime and postgame interviews sideline reporters conduct "helps you feel engaged," while another, Cole, stated, "I'd say if they're good at what they do, then they can be very useful." On the other hand, some informants felt the reports delivered by sideline reporters sometimes detract from their enjoyment of the telecast. "There are sometimes when I think they're just talking about pointless things when it's less related to the actual [game]," said Cindy, an undergraduate. She continued, "Sometimes I like it when [they report] about injuries or what's going on during the game. But when it's little outside things, I don't like it as much." It appears that sportscasting decision-makers must find a balance between not making sideline reporters too intrusive yet including them enough so as not to further diminish their credibility.

Patricia expressed a belief that the sideline reporter role was seen as a "throwaway role" primarily because it is a position in which women predominate. Given Lampley's comments, it stands to reason that the opinion that the sideline reporter is unnecessary may be a consequence of the role's original purpose *and* the gendered and racialized appearance double. The original purpose of the job, the appearance double standard, and an adherence to white feminine ideals have all therefore contributed to the construction of the concept of women sideline reporters as "cheerleaders with microphones."

Why Are There So Few Women in the Sportscasting Booth?

As it pertains to the paucity of women in the sportscasting booth for high-profile men's sports, I argue the constructed image of women sideline reporters as cheerleaders informs a neoliberal female sportscaster subjectivity by way of a "reassertion of sexual difference" (Gill 2007, 265)—in this case, the assumption that early-career and aspiring women sportscasters should want to be sideline reporters because the position caters to an ideal woman's strengths. The reassertion of sexual difference, which encourages women to be strategic about how they utilize their femininity to gain upward mobility only partly explains why there are so few women in the booth, however. Speaking with my informants and analyzing mass mediated texts made clear that the lack of women in the sportscasting booth is a complex issue, to the extent that there are a variety of explanations for the phenomenon. The complexity of the issue can make it difficult to pinpoint a cause or a solution. Among the explanations offered by my informants, an apparent lack of interest among aspiring women sportscasters most closely embodies a reassertion of sexual difference. Nevertheless, the historical predominance of men's voices in mediated sport and the industry's lack of intentionality in developing women announcers also inform the neoliberal female subjectivity. As they collectively place women at a disadvantage that remains unaddressed, these two explanations necessitate the usage of neoliberal (and thus entrepreneurial) logic among women who may aspire to be play-by-play announcers or color commentators for men's sports.

Women's Lack of Interest in the Play-by-Play Position

According to many of my interview informants, the paucity of women in the booth may owe to a lack of interest in those positions. Compared to the other two explanations following, this was the one most informed by gendered neoliberalism. While Nancy expressed a belief that "play-by-play is a skill that you can learn," she also said that it is a position to which few women seem to aspire. "For some reason, women don't want to go there, or I haven't seen it. All the letters I get, you know, or emails, that's not the role they want to pursue." The solution Nancy offered was purely neoliberal; according to her, although women have not been given equal opportunities to work in the broadcast booth, "they have to help themselves," given the lack of development that exists for such roles. Amelia supported the view that women could be more aggressive in pursuing roles in the broadcast booth if they want them. Having only recently taken an interest in doing play-by-play (to which she had yet to be assigned), she said, "I put it on myself. . . . I haven't pushed because I haven't put forth the necessary time to prepare myself and to get in on the ground."

Paula supported Nancy's and Amelia's assertion by positing that, if there are "one million men" who aspire to do play-by-play, "the reality is there's probably only 200,000 women who [want to do it]." Marie admitted that she has no interest in doing play-by-play but noted women in general may not be interested in the position because they are not groomed for that role early in their careers and because the role intimidates many women. She did suggest, however, that this lack of interest may change as more women enter the industry in general and the sportscasting booth in particular: "I think this new wave of women who are in sports media, younger than myself, the girls that are now watching me, they will have the confidence to say, 'Yeah, I can do that. I can be a play-by-play [announcer].'"

A young woman in one of my focus groups, Molly, intimated that the lack of women play-by-play announcers may result from a gendered predilection toward other roles *and* other industries: "A lot of people are willing to say, 'We want women, we want women.' I think sports as a whole is, yeah, a little bit more male-dominated, but there are also fields where it's female-dominated. And for men to come in, I don't think we would be talking about it in the same way we are with women." Molly makes the point that, as a society, we do not push quite as hard for more men to enter fields dominated by women—like nursing or elementary education—thus such an effort for equality in sportscasting is not necessary, if the interest from women is lacking.

The idea that positions in the booth are simply available to women if they want them—and that women naturally do not—is rooted in gendered neoliberalism's reassertion of sexual difference. Whereas so-called second-wave feminism emphasized the similarities between the sexes, it is now considered normal in the postfeminist era to point out or even embrace the "differences" between men and women. Molly's comments are therefore firmly grounded in gendered neoliberal discourse that has pervaded media culture from the late twentieth century. This discourse is seen often in "chick lit" or sitcoms (such as *The Big Bang Theory*), both of which have depicted men and women as possessing vastly different communication styles (among other things) and therefore not understanding each other (Gill 2007). This reaffirmation of difference is problematic to the extent that it has the potential to ignore the fact that the differences in question are discursively constructed through long-standing gendered messages and practices. That is, such differences between men and women likely exist because of socially constructed values that dictate what is normal for men and women, not because that difference occurs "naturally." These constructed notions are similar to the way the United States views athleticism along racialized lines; Blacks, especially Black men, are generally thought to be more naturally athletic than their white peers, based on unfounded claims of differences in bone structure and musculature among people of African descent. However, African Americans predominate most popular American sports because they have been encouraged—through representation and discourse—to participate in and master sports and have been similarly discouraged from participating in other, more intellectual pursuits (Carrington 2010, 174). Also, neoliberalism's call for personal responsibility willfully ignores the fact that, while men and women are equally likely to overlook certain professions, a long-standing set of practices might make it more difficult for women than men to choose a vocational path that bucks conventional norms.

The Predominance of Men's Voices

Among the aforementioned long-standing set of practices inhibiting the integration of women into the sportscasting booth is the predominance of men's voices in sports media products. The suggestion that sports media consumers, regardless of gender, are therefore unaccustomed to and averse to hearing women's voices throughout a sportscast was another explanation offered by my informants. Consider these comments made by Amelia:

> I think there's a reality of, do people *want* to hear a woman calling the game? That sounds really obvious, but I feel like a lot of people are afraid to say it. Do people want to hear a woman calling the game? I mean, some men might not. . . . But I think—here's the thing. There are a lot of networks out there that are doing it because they like the idea of it because it is different. And it's worth the try. Are you going to have a woman right now calling the Super Bowl? No, because I don't think we're there yet, and maybe we won't be there ever. I don't know.

According to Amelia, national sports networks have slowly integrated women—such as Beth Mowins and Jessica Mendoza—into the booth but are opposed to putting them in the most high-profile positions (allowing them to announce during the Super Bowl, for example) because sports media consumers are not "ready" to hear women's voices yet. If we equate audience readiness to acceptance, a look at mediated texts suggests there is validity to Amelia's assertion. When Mendoza made her Major League Baseball postseason debut as a sportscaster in October of 2015, Molly Knight (2015) compiled and disseminated via Twitter a series of tweets she saw criticizing Mendoza's presence in the telecast. Among the tweets she found, sent by men *and* women:

> sos, there's a woman talking during my baseball watching

ESPN putting a woman broadcaster in the booth for a playoff baseball games is one of their worst decisions ever.

The last thing I want to hear while I'm watching baseball is a woman talking.

What's a woman doing on the play by play broadcast team for a MLB game??? Unacceptable!!! That's a sell out!!!

For these sports media consumers, Mendoza's skills and knowledge in the booth was not the issue. Instead, she did not belong in the booth simply because she is a woman. As Julie DiCaro (2017) wrote in an op-ed for the *New York Times*, Mowins faced similarly sexist criticism upon making her *Monday Night Football* debut. However, the criticisms curated by DiCaro focused on Mowins's voice:

Hey @espn, I commend you for giving Beth Mowins a shot.. but her voice is annoying to listen to.

Beth mowins voice super annoying. Please replace immediately.

I'm sure Beth Mowins is a nice person but her voice should not be on tv. I feel like she is scolding me for throwing snowballs.

Other comments made about women sportscasters' voices, as cited by DiCaro, suggest that listening to them is "like listening to my ex nag me" (para. 3) and they "sound like mom yelling at me" (para. 4). A sportscaster's vocal tone is a significant aspect of an announcer's ability to attract and hold an audience; as such, these may be well-founded critiques. Nevertheless, the available discourse demonstrates that, as opposed to women's voices legitimately not being "right" for live commentary, criticism of women's voices in sportscasting may be rooted in a social construct that discursively situates their voices as inappropriate for the booth. As veteran sports reporter Andrea Kremer told DiCaro in the same op-ed, "I have no doubt that 'hating the sound of her voice' is code for 'I hate that there was a woman announcing football'" (para. 10). This is not to say that women announcers should not be judged by their voices; men sportscasters are subject to the same scrutiny. However, Kremer suggested that scrutiny of women's voices is often rooted in a gendered bias that has been constructed over time. The inability for scholars and sports media personalities alike to decipher which criticisms are founded and which are sexist adds to the contentiousness of this debate. It also demonstrates the subjective nature of our evaluations of sportscaster talent. Nevertheless, while criticism of a woman's voice is not always sexist, it often is.

In explaining why sports media consumers generally disapprove of women's voices inside the broadcast booth, one of my focus group informants, Marcus, lent credence to the possibility that sports media consumers do not find woman's voices suitable because they find them to be similar to those of their mothers and spouses. "It's like, 'Oh, my gosh. She's like my wife or something.' It's like, 'I don't want to think about my wife while I'm trying to relax *away* from my wife.'" This view assumes, again, that heterosexual men are the primary audience, even though many women—who represent half of the sports media consumer base (DiCaro 2020)—also take issue with women's voices. Marcus's comments also assume that all men in significant heterosexual relationships are "nagged" by their partners and that these men watch sports to distance themselves from their partners or from women in general. Because these assumptions are dubious, it is difficult to reject Kremer's assertion that sports media consumers usually disapprove of women's voices because they disapprove of their very presence during the telecast of a sporting event.

It is likely that sports media consumers also repudiate women's voices because they are simply not accustomed to hearing women provide play-by-play or color commentary, considering the long-standing invisibility of women in those roles. Even the most open-minded sports fan can be taken aback when hearing a woman provide commentary. Consider this perspective from Patricia:

> I really don't think that it's acceptable to the majority of the masses to hear a woman calling play-by-play. . . . It would be strange for *me* to even hear, and I am a woman in sports [media]. But I feel that it would be jarring to me to hear a woman's voice calling play-by-play just because it's just something that hasn't really been done. It's been done a few times, of course, but not enough—when you tune in you expect to hear a deep male voice calling the game and telling you what's going on. That's just

kind of the way things have been. And I think that that's one area where sports viewers, men and women alike, are not willing to budge.

Paula supported this view by stating, "That's just what we have been programmed to like or know, is a male voice behind a mic. . . . We have not been programmed to hear a woman." The "programming" Paula speaks of hides in plain sight; it is visible yet unspoken and it is neither intentional nor explicit. Parents, for example, generally do not tell their children that only men can be play-by-play announcers or color commentators—at least not for the purpose of priming their media consumption.

The way sports are documented and historicized, through archival footage and audio clips, adds to women's invisibility in the booth. Due to the long-standing lack of representation of women in the booth—reinforced whenever any of American sports' most prominent moments are revisited in radio, television, or film products—sports media consumers usually hear men's voices. "It's like that," Paula said, "because that's just how it is, and this has been since, shit, before TV, when it was just the radio, back in the day. It's always been males calling games." In sum, the predominance of men's voices in the sportscasting booth has primed sports media consumers to expect to hear men while consuming sports media products. Over time, this expectation has become an obstacle that the neoliberal female sportscaster subject must overcome, either by transcending that obstacle à la Beth Mowins or by avoiding it altogether. The sustained avoidance of the play-by-play position by aspiring women sportscasters—as corroborated by Nancy and Marie—has been encouraged both by the lack of women's voices in live sporting event coverage *and* a lack of developmental opportunities for women.

Hiring and Development Bias

The exclusion of women's voices from sports' most well-documented moments, and women's avoidance of the play-by-play and color commentary roles, has informed the assumption by some media consumers and industry decision-makers that men are more naturally suited for those roles in men's sports coverage. A bias against hiring women for such roles is therefore manifest in the efforts (or the lack thereof) taken by the industry to develop women for those positions. This supports Nancy's and Amelia's assertions that women must be more aggressive in their pursuit of such roles, if that is what they desire. In explaining why she believed there to be relatively little interest in those positions among women, in addition to her contention that play-by-play can be intimidating, Marie added, "I think that it's because as women were coming up the ranks earlier on, it was just like, 'Okay, this is going to be your role. You're going to be the host or you're going to be the sideline reporter.'" In other words, women who aspired to be sportscasters were pigeonholed into a small number of positions earmarked for women.

In discussing the color analyst role for men's sports—which is usually given to former men athletes—the views provided by my informants were split. Some women, like Nancy, believed that analyst roles for sports like football, which has no intercollegiate or professional women's equivalent on par with the NFL, should go to the people who have played or coached the sport, on the grounds that they are most well equipped to explain for the audience what exactly they are seeing on the field. "I think the reason I lasted all these years," Nancy said, "is I never pretended that I knew what [my color analyst] knew. I wasn't in the huddle." Similarly, Paula believed that the best chance a woman has at getting into the broadcast booth for high-profile men's sports is if they were a former athlete and became a color analyst for a women's sport, like Doris Burke, who played collegiate basketball at Providence College before becoming a women's basketball analyst. Being an athlete is not viewed as an asset for play-by-play announcers, however—in fact, most did not play their sports at an elite level. Nevertheless, women still are not afforded equitable opportunities to pursue play-by-play, and, without the privileged perspective of being former elite athletes, women therefore have a slimmer chance than men of entering the booth. Hannah believes that even former women athletes encounter bias for men's sports analyst positions, even if they played the women's equivalent of the same sport. "The woman—she could have been in the WNBA—and they're like, 'Well no, it's still not the NBA; so, why would she be as knowledgeable about the NBA, compared to a man?'" As of this writing, there are three full-time women television analysts in the NBA, and all three of them played basketball at the collegiate level, if not professionally. Still, Hannah's point, that former women athletes generally face bias when seeking analyst positions for men's sports still stands, as evidenced by the sexist criticism launched at Jessica Mendoza, if we accept softball as a close enough equivalent to baseball.

Conversely, Lizzy and Stephanie both questioned the notion that only a former athlete—man or woman—would be qualified to be an analyst. In truth, while it is rare, national networks have not been averse to hiring as analysts men who have little to no collegiate or professional playing experience. From 2000 through 2002, ABC Sports employed comedian Dennis Miller as a color commentator during its *Monday Night Football* telecasts. In 2003 ESPN—long owned by the same companies (Capital Cities and then Disney) that owned ABC—hired conservative political commentator Rush Limbaugh as an analyst for its *Sunday NFL Countdown* pregame show. From 2006 to 2008, ESPN used Tony Kornheiser, a sportswriter and cohost of ESPN's *Pardon the Interruption*, as an analyst for *Monday Night Football*. Kornheiser's role was perceived by many observers to be similar to that of Miller's—a comedic voice in the booth who spoke for the common fan and could also provide tidbits of information. Finally, from 2014 through the end of the 2015 Major League Baseball season, FOX Sports employed Tom Verducci, a longtime sportswriter for *Sports Illustrated*, as an analyst. He was given the opportunity to provide commentary during the World Series in both years. Although the list of names is short, networks have shown a willingness to permit men who were never elite athletes into the broadcast booth as analysts. Rare as it has been for men on television, this is an opportunity that has only been, as stated previously, afforded to an even smaller number of women who were not elite athletes. Even then, these women have mostly provided analysis for men's sports on radio (Lesley Visser) and on alternate audio channels of internet video streams (Andrea Kremer)—discursively signifying their insights as not normal.

Media organizations' willingness and ability to hire announcers who are not former elite athletes at least demonstrates that being hired to be an analyst does not require privileged knowledge. Stephanie agrees: "I do like [the analyst for the team I cover]. Just for the record, I think he's fine, but I don't think he comes up with anything that I couldn't come up with. . . . Half the time I say the same thing he's saying at the same time he's saying it, and it's usually something to do with how much dirt a pitcher has on his uniform. My sister could notice that and she doesn't watch sports." This is not to say privileged knowledge is not valuable to sports media consumers. Instead, Stephanie's comment suggests that privileged knowledge is not always a requisite for what constitutes acceptable analysis.

Stephanie went further in discussing the lack of women in the booth overall, for both play-by-play and analyst positions, explaining that a bias against women precludes them from getting opportunities to develop the skills required by those roles. "God knows I don't think it's because women aren't interested or because women aren't qualified," she said, before comparing the situation to the development of women baseball players: "Why can't a woman pitcher throw ninety-six miles an hour? Well, if you don't develop her from the start, if you assume that it's a foregone conclusion she's never going to get there, even if she turns out to be six-three and can deadlift six of me, if you didn't develop her as a player from the time she was five years old like you do for the guys, she's going to become a softball player, and of course she's never going to be able to throw ninety-six." In other words, if women are not afforded the opportunity to develop as play-by-play announcers or analysts and are instead assumed to be unsuitable for—or uninterested in—these positions, then women will prepare and develop the skills required for careers that are more available to them. Just as softball is more available to women athletes than baseball, sideline reporting, anchoring and hosting are all more available for women sportscasters than are positions in the booth.

Conclusion

The sex bias in the hiring and retention of women sportscasters generally, and women play-by-play announcers and color commentators specifically, informs and is informed by the neoliberal female sportscaster subjectivity. On one hand, this bias has become another obstacle that aspiring women sportscasters are expected to either overcome with little institutional support (by way of intentional training and development) or avoid altogether, often on the grounds that women are not "built" for these positions. On the other hand, the expectation that women navigate this obstacle is the result of the gendered and racialized, neoliberal standards of beauty and temperament that also construct the female sportscaster subject. Stated another way, women have had difficulty integrating sportscasting's "glass booth" because of the status quo, and because women haven't equitably integrated the booth, the status quo is reinforced. In keeping with gendered neoliberal discourse, the process of maintaining this status quo is also paradoxical, insofar as women's attempts to pursue play-by-play and analyst roles are stymied by assumptions that they are not initially interested or later well-suited for such roles. Gendered neoliberalism therefore presents women sportscasters with a catch-22 whereby they are generally not provided the opportunity to demonstrate and develop a passion and a talent for such roles.

The analysis of both the industry's double standards and sex bias in hiring and retention demonstrates the impact gendered neoliberalism has on the everyday, material experiences of women sportscasters. Also apparent is the reliance of the industry's gendered structure—in which women generally remain on the sidelines—on gendered neoliberalism. As women have been left to their own devices to navigate these challenges, and have done so successfully, neoliberal discourse normalizes these obstacles, desensitizing us to them. After all, the logic goes, if an Erin Andrews can make it big and if a Doris Burke and Jessica Mendoza can obtain analysts roles for high-profile men's sports, the situation must not be that dire. However, gendered neoliberalism does more than normalize expectations that govern woman sportscaster appearance, development, and upward mobility. As I argue in chapter 3, the normalized expectations placed on the neoliberal female sportscaster subject also inform and are informed by gendered harassment. As a result, women sportscasters are in a precarious position, one in which their physical and mental wellbeing are squarely at risk.

THREE

Gendered Offline and Online Harassment in Sportscasting

Due to the #MeToo movement, 2017 will long be remembered as the year that brought to light a culture that allows (mostly) men to harass, humiliate, fondle, and even rape women—and, to a lesser extent, men—with impunity. Despite the attention given to #MeToo, the media narrative on sexual misconduct often misses the forest for the trees. As Sarah Banet-Weiser (2017, para. 2) wrote for *Fortune*, "The media focus has been on highly visible celebrity men—those men who occupy important positions of power. . . . The news stories emphasize the individuals involved rather than the structural underpinning of all these industries." Although men in the entertainment (Harvey Weinstein), news media (Matt Lauer), sports (Larry Nassar), and political (Donald Trump) arenas dominated the headlines, accusations and subsequent disciplinary actions taken against personnel at ESPN and the NFL Network show that the sports media were also complicit in a system that has long ignored sexual misconduct. In the sportscasting industry, as in politics, news, and entertainment, the effect of sexual harassment on its "structural underpinning" has been similarly underreported. It is in this vein that chapter 3 approaches the topic of gendered harassment in sportscasting and its mutually informing relationship with the neoliberal female sportscaster subjectivity.

In this chapter, I examine the ways misconduct such as online and offline sexual harassment informs and is informed by gendered neoliberalism, its construction of the female sportscaster subjectivity, and the gendered structure of the sportscasting industry. I argue that much of the harassment women sportscasters endure is rooted in gendered neoliberal discourse. This argument sets the stage for chapter 4, in which I explain how the expectation that women manage this harassment on their own is also grounded in gendered neoliberalism. Furthermore, sexual harassment in sportscasting is, in large part, informed by sportscasting's gendered and racialized double standards and bias in hiring and development, both of which are supported by gendered neoliberal logic. Both phenomena have resulted in a view of women sportscasters that, while rife with contradiction, excludes most women who do not conform to a sexualized Anglocentric feminine ideal, a view that also generally marginalizes women sportscaster opinions. Women in the industry are therefore objectified by default. Finally, I argue that sportscasting's gendered harassment has a material impact on the industry's hierarchy insofar as that harassment ensures that men continue to dominate the industry and occupy a preponderance of sportscasting's most prominent positions. To advance these arguments, I analyze two sites of harassment: the sportscasting workplace, within which exists sexual harassment, as defined and as regulated by U.S. federal anti-discrimination laws, and the online environment, which has not yet been so closely regulated.

As is the case for double standards and sex bias, harassment is a phenomenon that is not unique to sportscasting nor is it new in this contemporary moment. In examining harassment, this chapter therefore further contextualizes another long-standing, socially embedded, and normalized practice within the sportscasting industry, its mutually informing relationship with the neoliberal female sportscaster subjectivity, and its impact on the gendered structure of the sportscasting industry.

Workplace Harassment

Due in part to the prevalence of online harassment, as highlighted by the Peabody Award–winning "#MoreThanMean" public service announcement, the workplace harassment of women working in the sportscasting industry had not been extensively reported in the twenty-first century until the #MeToo movement in late 2017. Nevertheless, there are enough available contemporary narratives surrounding workplace sexual harassment to conclude that it is informed by the neoliberal female sportscaster subjectivity, insofar as that harassment is a phenomenon informed by sportscasting's gendered and racialized double standards and bias in hiring and development, all of which are buttressed by gendered neoliberalism.

Although workplace sexual harassment in sports media has been overshadowed by that in the online realm in recent decades, the harassment of women working in sports media of course predates the twenty-first century. In previous decades, as the participation and interest in sports among women increased, the issue of locker room access for women sports journalists surfaced as the most significant site of women's subordination within the sports media industry. The issue first gained national attention in 1978 when Melissa Ludtke, then a writer for *Sports Illustrated*, was denied access to the New York Yankees locker room during the World Series. She successfully filed a civil rights lawsuit for the right to conduct interviews in the "males only" clubhouse (Boutilier and SanGiovanni 1983). For many years after the court's ruling, "access did not mean acceptance" (Creedon 1998, 93).

Alison Gordon of the *Toronto Star*, for instance, became the first woman beat writer for an American League baseball team when she took the position and covered the Toronto Blue Jays in 1979. In her memoir, she wrote of a team official giving her a t-shirt that read "Token Broad Beat Writer" and players in the clubhouse greeting her with shouts of "Pecker Checker" (Gordon 1984, 121–23). Susan Fornoff (1993) covered the Oakland Athletics for five years as a writer for the *Sacramento Bee*. During her time as the Athletics' beat writer, she determined she had two choices: distance herself from the athletes she was covering or assimilate to their culture and socialize with them. In determining that assimilation was her best course of action, Fornoff made herself more susceptible to direct harassment. The hostile environment that she then experienced, which included incessant harassment from famed slugger Dave Kingman, was what eventually "drove [her] away from sportswriting" (227).

Perhaps the most infamous case of harassment committed against a woman sports journalist in the locker room is that of Lisa Olson and the New England Patriots of the National Football League in 1990. Olson was the Patriots' beat writer for the *Boston Herald* when members of the team sexually harassed her in the locker room while she was conducting an interview. While Olson (1990, 74) conducted her interview at a player's locker, multiple Patriots attempted to distract her by suggestively displaying—and commenting on—their genitalia. The harassment had its desired effect; Olson left the locker room before concluding her interview. She later described the encounter as an act of "mind rape" that left her feeling "humiliated and degraded" (Kane and Disch 1993, 332). In the incident's aftermath, the *Boston Globe* reported the story, opening a wave of news coverage that included a *Herald* story quoting then–Patriots owner Victor Kiam as calling Olson a "classic bitch." For the remainder of 1990 and into 1991, Boston-area sports fans harassed Olson even after she was reassigned to cover the Boston Bruins of the National Hockey League during the 1990 NFL season. To escape the harassment, Olson was eventually reassigned to one of the *Herald*'s sister publications in Australia.

Though the issue of women's access to men's locker rooms was seemingly resolved by the mid-1990s, the harassment of women working in sports media has not ceased. In speaking with my informants and reviewing narratives available in the public press, I found there to be three primary manifestations of workplace harassment against women in sportscasting: hostile work environments, quid pro quo, and stalking, with each manifestation informed by both gendered neoliberal discourse and, to varying degrees, by the industry's double standards and bias.

Hostile Work Environment and the Reproductive Paradox

As it relates to hostile work environment harassment, women in sportscasting are often treated by media organizations as liabilities simply because of their ability to bear children. This view of women in the industry often creates a work environment that once again presents narrow and contradictory boundaries. In this case, women must closely adhere to the Anglocentric feminine traits examined in chapter 1—including a nurturing, stereotypically motherlike temperament—while also demonstrating no ability to procreate. These boundaries make it taboo for women to have or exhibit signs of female reproduction, including menstruation, pregnancy, and miscarriage. This reproductive taboo is supported by neoliberal, postfeminist discourse, to the extent that such discourse in this case co-opts the feminist notion that women do not have to be homemakers in the service of the antifeminist idea that women sportscasters should refrain from having children.

Among my informants, both Marie and Paula admitted to experiencing harassment in the form of a hostile work environment. According to the United States Equal Employment Opportunity Commission (2018, para. 2), hostile work environment harassment is a form of discrimination that occurs when a person engages in "unwanted conduct" that is based on race, sex, religion, and many other protected classes or groups. To be unlawful, the conduct must be pervasive enough "to create a work environment that would be intimidating, hostile, or offensive to reasonable people" (para. 3). For instance, Marie had a particularly rocky working relationship with a sports director she used to work with.[1] She knew going into the job that he was "kind of a weird guy," but she took the job, her first out of college, because she needed the income and experience. According to Marie, it only took a few weeks before she was the target of the sports director's strange behavior. "He asked me when my period was so he could track when I was going to get it and when I was PMSing so that he would know that I was going to be moody." Twenty-two years old at the time, Marie did not say anything to anyone at the station because she felt she was too new to file a complaint. Feeling she had not accumulated the social capital necessary to accuse her sports director of harassment, Marie continued to have what she described as a "terrible relationship" with him, one in which there would be minimal interaction between them, save for the occasional instance in which he would purposely intimidate Marie. "We had a radio booth and whenever he wanted to talk to me, he would basically kind of trap me in there and block the door." Over time, it became clear to Marie the sports director was gruff with many of the station's employees, regardless of gender. Upon eventually telling her regional manager about her sports director's harassment, she discovered that the director was "on his last legs." When the station made the decision to fire him, he had already accepted a job offer in another market. Although the sports director harassed both male and female colleagues, his interactions with Marie served to assert his superiority over her as a man and—given his remarks about Marie's menstrual cycle—stigmatize certain aspects of her femininity.

Journeywoman sportscaster Lindsay McCormick reportedly faced another reproductive stigma during a job interview for the NFL Network. During the interview, McCormick was allegedly asked if she "plan[ned] on getting knocked up immediately like the rest of them," if she was hired (Martin 2017, para. 2). Former *SportsCenter* anchor Lindsay Czarniak chose to walk away from ESPN after the network offered her a different job with a significant pay cut upon her return from maternity leave. Not only are these actions violations of the Family Medical Leave Act of 1993, but the reference in McCormick's case to "the rest of them" carries with it an assumption that women in general are liabilities simply due to their potential to procreate. The stigmatization of femininity marks women sportscasters' bodies as always already unruly, in need of constant monitoring, lest they explicitly show a capacity to procreate, as during pregnancy. This reproductive taboo can create an atmosphere, such as the one reported by the *Boston Globe* (Abelson 2017), in which women sportscasters hide pregnancies and even miscarriages. Such was the case for Sara Walsh who, while working at ESPN, elected to go on the air despite bleeding after a miscarriage to hide it from her colleagues and superiors (para. 47).

The stigmatization of female reproductive activity within the industry contradicts the white feminine ideals that call on women to demonstrate a capacity to nurture men as well as children (Deliovsky 2010). In this contradiction's case, though the standards for "good" motherhood continue to evolve, broadly speaking, how can a woman present herself as stereotypically motherly if she must also hide her ability to reproduce? Although it seems impossible that a woman might present herself as hyperfeminine but not *that* feminine, there is evidence that women sportscasters must comply with the pressure of hiding pregnancies if they are to demonstrate their reliability. According to the *Boston Globe* report (Abelson 2017), many women in the industry, like Lindsay Czarniak, are effectively replaced—often by other women—upon returning from maternity leave. This practice of replacing women with women demonstrates that hiring women sportscasters, regardless of their plans to procreate, is not actually detrimental to sports media organizations. There seems to be a steady enough labor force from which the industry can (un)lawfully recruit replacements for the women who decide to start or add to their families.

This reality calls into question the logic behind the reproductive paradox in sportscasting; why does the industry discourage women from procreating if those women can be so readily replaced, and by other women, no less? It may be that media organizations are averse to hiring and on-boarding temporary replacements, due to the inconvenience that task presents to producers. It could also be a desire to maintain continuity among on-air talent, which may or may not have an impact on ratings. Even if it were legal, the practice of questioning a woman about her reproductive plans during an interview, or fostering an environment in which she feels compelled to hide a miscarriage, is nevertheless rendered unnecessary. Applying Occam's Razor, misogyny is likely the best, most accurate explanation for why this practice exists; such a practice is a convenient way to curb women's upward mobility and empowerment in sportscasting, ensuring they remain on the margins of the industry as a result.

As has been stated throughout this book, phenomena such as the reproductive paradox are not unique to nor solely informed by norms within sportscasting. Much like the appearance double standard and the expectations placed on women regarding their self-presentation, socially embedded taboos of menstruation, miscarriage, and pregnancy are present in other social institutions. However, as is the case with the appearance double standard and its paradox, the aforementioned taboos are manifest in a way that is less generalizable to society at large. The appearance double standard paradox is the result of a clash between the taken-for-granted, antifeminist norms of an industry in which appearance is of great import and seemingly feminist standards for "appropriate" dress. Likewise, the paradox that calls on women sportscasters to adhere to Anglocentric feminine ideals until they get pregnant is linked to a clash undergirded by the gendered and racialized appearance double standard. In chapter 1 I wrote that women sportscasters are expected to look and dress sexy but could be deemed to look or dress *too* sexy to be decent or credible. Here, if a woman's sexiness is correlated in some measure to her femininity, it seems women sportscasters need to be feminine insofar as they look sexy but not so feminine as to exhibit a physical capacity for motherhood. That is, a woman sportscaster is expected to look and behave like a (white) woman but work like a stereotypically masculine man while doing it. Furthermore, this paradox presents another postfeminist entanglement of feminist and antifeminist discourses. In this case, the idea that women can choose work over child-rearing and "homemaking" is rooted in second-wave feminism, but that idea is co-opted to advance the antifeminist practice of employers discouraging or not retaining women who either get pregnant or might want to. As a result of this postfeminist discourse and its mutually informing relationship with the industry's double standards and bias, the female sportscaster reproductive paradox therefore contributes to the construction of the neoliberal female sportscaster subjectivity.

Quid Pro Quo

The quid pro quo—or *this for that*—harassment of women sportscasters is also the result of a neoliberal mode of representation that prioritizes Anglocentric white femininity over talent and knowledge. Presenting women reporters first and foremost as sexual objects, or postfeminist desiring subjects who are seemingly always up for sex while on the job, places all of the industry's women, regardless of their method of self-presentation, in a precarious situation when they engage male sources to report sports news. Not only does quid pro quo harassment create another type of hostile work environment if the woman sportscaster rejects a source's sexual advances; it also undergirds the subordination of women in sports media by precluding many of those women from producing the type of stories for which their male counterparts earn upward mobility and acclaim. When certain sources such as male athletes and coaches view women in the industry as objects meant to fulfill their amorous or sexual desires, women sportscasters become reluctant to fully pursue leads from those sources.

Early in her career, Paula experienced a hostile work environment after a college football player she covered, one of the most popular on his team, propositioned her for a date. Upon rejecting him, the player called her a bitch, gave curt responses during interviews, and spread rumors that she had been sleeping with his teammates. As Paula clarified, athletes and coaches sometimes ostracize men reporters, too, but that usually occurs in response to a report the male journalist wrote or gave on television. Instead, this player turned on Paula because she did not agree to go on a date with him. Getting propositioned by athletes, Paula said, is still commonplace for her, despite now being married and covering a professional football team. "I always get hit on by the rookies until other people are like, 'She's married. Just don't try. We've tried. Don't try.' And it's just kind of frustrating." According to Paula, coaches also behave this way, though they often act professionally at first before later making an advance. As a result of what she believes to be her male sources' always-present desire for sex, she stated that she has never had a strictly platonic interaction with a male source.

Aside from the emotional consequences of Paula's experiences, there are also vocational implications to consider regarding the role sexual harassment occupies in structuring gendered power and access in sportscasting as an institution. These sorts of interactions can make it challenging for women sports journalists to obtain information for stories that their male colleagues can get without the expectation of dates or sexual favors in return. As one unnamed reporter told *Sports Illustrated*'s Richard Deitsch (2017, para. 32), there is always "information to be had—for the right price," she said. "The implication is always clear, always just beneath the surface. . . . As competitive and as driven as I am, there have actually been moments in my career where I had to be OK with taking an 'L' [and letting a story go] because it wasn't worth dealing with the nonsense." This was the tack taken by Amelia Rayno, former *Star Tribune* reporter who covered the University of Minnesota. Though it limited the number of "scoops" she might have been be able to uncover as a journalist, Rayno (2015) stopped all non-essential communication with UM's then-director of athletics Norwood Teague when he continued to make unwanted advances toward her. In response, he continued to send her text messages that included statements such as "U seem obtuse" and "Ur giving me a complex" (para. 18). In this instance, not only did Teague seek an amorous relationship with Rayno but, after getting rebuffed, requested that she nurture his damaged ego. Although Rayno is a print journalist, Teague's request tracks with the white feminine ideals of comportment that are expected of women sportscasters.

After Rayno asked for him to stop his advances, Teague's behavior evolved into stalking, a third type of workplace sexual harassment.

Stalking

Like quid pro quo, stalking is also a symptom of an appearance double standard that is buttressed by neoliberalism and broadly diminishes the female sportscaster's perceived credibility, informing the perception that women are solely hired for the aesthetic and physical pleasure of heterosexual male sports media consumers, media managers, and sports news sources. In addition, stalking, along with quid pro quo, force women in the industry to confront another dilemma that, while having no desirable choices, also serves the construction of the ideal neoliberal female sportscaster subject.

One woman sportscaster I spoke with, Hannah, believed her perceived lack of credibility caused a man to ignore her abilities and responsibilities as a journalist as he developed and exhibited an obsession with her. Hannah's experience also showed that women are often required to cover men who had previously behaved inappropriately toward them or toward other women reporters. An assistant coach of a team Hannah once covered stalked her by continuing to send her messages on social media despite her requests that the messages cease. She thought the messages started innocently enough, including comments like "Hey, pretty girl." However, the coach started asking her what she was doing on weekends and where she lived before demanding that she see him outside their professional relationship. When she blocked his Facebook and Twitter accounts, he used his employer's Twitter account to continue his advances.

When Hannah reported the stalking to the sports director at her station, he approached the team's head coach, who saw to it that the stalking ended. Although the head coach was embarrassed, he admitted that Hannah was not the first reporter to be propositioned by his assistant. Making matters worse, in Hannah's view, was the fact that her sports director obliged the head coach's impassioned request to have her continue to cover their games: "[Despite] how uncomfortable I felt, and how much I asked him not to send me to these games, he sent me, literally, every other day for two weeks straight to cover this team."

Similar to the way the appearance double standard diminishes women sportscasters' perceived credibility, the quid quo pro harassment and stalking of women sportscasters serves to discursively subordinate women in the industry. Women caught in such situations face another double bind: They can choose not to interact with a source who the reporter knows will expect a date or sexual favors in return and risk being replaced or watch a male colleague cash in on a story that could have advanced her career or improved the status of women in the industry overall. Or these women can choose to interact with the harassing source and risk humiliation and shame (or worse) during and after the interaction. This double bind is another in a group of dilemmatic choices women sportscasters are often forced to make and illuminates the effect sexual harassment can have on sportscasting's gendered hierarchy. More relevant to this book's theme, however, is the fact that this harassment also bolsters the industry's construction of the ideal neoliberal female sportscaster subject. In this case, those women who can (seemingly) successfully navigate harassment on their own and produce good stories despite their sources' behavior are viewed as ideally suited for this industry. Those women who choose not to navigate harassment—either by not pursuing certain stories or leaving the industry altogether—are viewed as not having the chops to make it as reporters.

The stories Marie (hostile work environment), Paula (quid pro quo), and Hannah (stalking) shared are far from the only harassment each has had to endure, but they are the most egregious cases they recalled. The experiences they shared suggest that there is a relationship between sexual misconduct in sports media and the double standards examined in chapter 1, whereby the former is largely informed by the latter. "It almost makes me feel like they're undermining my [credibility]," Hannah said. "Like, 'Oh, because she's a woman, I can speak to her this way.' . . . So, it kind of makes me feel like my [credibility] has been taken away a little bit, because they don't see me as anything more than just a face, so to speak." That is, the industry's prioritization of looks for women sportscasters, at the expense of their perceived credibility as journalists, seems to have contributed to an environment in which some women sportscasters are primarily viewed by some media consumers and sources as sexual trophies to be won.

This environment marks many women sportscasters as potential objects of sexual desire first and journalists second, regardless of what they wear or how much makeup the have on. Marking women sportscasters in this manner is especially dangerous given socially embedded attitudes that celebrate, or at the very least condone, the notion that "boys will be boys"—in this case, the excessive, endless, and supposedly natural pursuit of sexual partners—which contributes to rape culture. In the context of sportscasting, the dangers of an emphasis on looks therefore echo the dangers of the postfeminist turn from sexual object to "desiring sexual subject," that women are presented as being "always up for it" (Gill 2007, 259). In examining my informants' experiences, sportscasting's de-emphasis on women sportscasters' ability and knowledge, therefore, has much to do with the prevalence of sexual quid pro quo and stalking within the industry.

Online Harassment

Due in large part to the 2016 "#MoreThanMean" public service announcement, in which sportscasters Julie DiCaro and Sarah Spain have malicious tweets read to them by "average" men who did not send the tweets, the online harassment of women working in sports media has been well documented and well known. While many women sports journalists have gone on the record as having mostly positive experiences online, those same women have also said that even the relatively small number of negative experiences they have online causes emotional distress and self-doubt (Everbach 2018). Furthermore, the online environment has become increasingly problematic for women sportscasters as the maintenance of a social media presence has become part of a sportscaster's duties (Laucella 2014). While the existence of online harassment against women sports journalists has been widely documented in recent years, what is less known are the various forms that harassment takes and how they function as another form of oppression that informs the construction of the neoliberal female sportscaster. The cause of this harassment is, of course, misogyny, but as it relates to the neoliberal female sportscaster subjectivity, online harassment also serves to legitimize the industry's dependence on gendered neoliberalism.

Here, I analyze two distinct—but often overlapping—types of gendered online harassment in sportscasting. The first type, an extension of the credibility double standard, occurs in response to female sportscaster opinions; women in the industry sometimes receive death and rape threats for simply expressing their opinions. This phenomenon especially manifests itself if a woman sportscaster says anything that would suggest a lapse in judgment by or a character flaw in a popular male athlete. The second type of online harassment is that which objectifies or sexualizes a woman sportscaster. Much like quid pro quo and stalking, the appearance and credibility double standards undergird the online objectification and sexualization of women in sportscasting. Because of the inequitable prioritization of appearance in the hiring and retention of women sportscasters, women in the industry have found themselves and their bodies to be the subjects of scrutiny and sexual fantasy. In some instances, the two types of online harassment have overlapped; internet users have objectified women sportscasters as a way of discrediting and silencing their opinions. Together, these forms of online harassment are informed by gendered neoliberalism, through the postfeminist entanglements and contradictions often found within those forms of harassment.

Furthermore, the online harassment of women sportscasters is rooted in popular misogyny. In general, the ceaseless gender-based online harassment that twenty-first-century Western women often endure "is not just due to scattered instances of boys being boys" (Banet-Weiser 2018, 84). Instead, gendered online harassment is a "manifestation of a popular misogyny that has grown alongside the growth of popular feminism." That is, as feminism has become networked, popularized, and readily championed by capitalistic organizations, misogyny has become similarly networked, popularized, and readily championed, though perhaps to a lesser extent. Popular misogyny serves as a response for men (and sometimes women) who believe that, because of popular feminism, men can no longer enjoy the full range of vocational, recreational, and sexual opportunities and liberties previously afforded to them. In other words, men feel as though they "have been made to feel shame in being men" (Banet-Weiser 2018, 84). This response is not unique to the twenty-first century; misogyny has long sought to delegitimize feminist politics. What is unique to the contemporary moment, however, is the usage of digital networked media to disseminate this response. To wit, I also analyze one such example of popular misogyny: FOX Sports personality Clay Travis's response to the "#MoreThanMean" PSA, which exemplified Banet-Weiser's (2018) concept of popular misogyny's funhouse mirror, a means of parroting yet distorting mediated feminist products so as to delegitimize them.

As a result of the rise of popular misogyny, and much like the workplace harassments examined previously, the online harassment of women sportscasters serves to keep women—ever encroaching on so-called masculine territory—on the periphery of the sportscasting industry. This subordination is a two-step cycle rooted in gendered neoliberalism: in the first step, an ad-hominem attack as harassment occurs. That is, as a result of the industry's neoliberal double standards and bias, some aspect of the woman sportscaster's character or identity as a woman is attacked, rather than or in addition to the argument or opinion she shares. In the second step, in response to the harassment, women in sportscasting are forced to choose between performing and not performing the affective labor, or emotion management, required to fulfill their usual job duties. While I explore the first step in this chapter, the cycle's second step—affective labor—is the focus of chapter 4. Together, this cycle not only serves to silence women in the industry but also legitimizes the sportscasting industry's dependence on gendered neoliberalism vis-à-vis the treatment of women sportscasters. Without conforming to and employing the neoliberal logics that dictate that women sportscasters navigate harassment with little to no meaningful institutional assistance, women sportscasters cannot thrive in or perhaps even enter the industry. Furthermore, those women who do navigate harassment are seen as successful and thriving, demonstrating gendered neoliberalism's effectiveness as a coping mechanism for women in the industry.

The Result of Expressing Opinions

Based on a reading of the interviews I conducted and the mediated texts I analyzed, the primary medium through which women in the industry receive backlash for expressing their opinions in the twenty-first century is, unsurprisingly, social media in general and Twitter in particular. This form of online harassment is primarily informed by popular misogyny but is also informed by the white feminine ideals that govern women sportscaster temperament, insofar as a woman must always be happy and nurturing. Lizzy recalled an occasion in which she was harassed on Twitter after offering her opinion of NFL quarterback Cam Newton's taciturn approach to a press conference immediately after his team's loss in Super Bowl 50. In addition to being called "all sorts of horrific names," the fantasy sports show host received death threats, simply for saying she believed Newton's behavior was "childish." In 2014 ESPN reporter and host Sam Ponder criticized the sports blogosphere for what she saw as hypocrisy in the wake of the NFL's handling of Ray Rice's domestic violence. "Blogs/websites that constantly disrespect women & objectify their bodies, then take a strong stand on the Ray Rice issue really confuse me," she tweeted (Ponder 2014). In response, Ponder received a wave of demeaning tweets, including:

[This is] the dumbest thing on Twitter I've read in weeks. Congrats. Your entire career is based on being good looking.

[H]ey Sam, you're hot and NOBODY gives a fuck what you say. Not even ya husband. (Yoder 2014b, emphasis in original)

Lizzy's and Ponder's experiences track with Julie DiCaro's (2015, para. 2) argument, referenced in chapter 1, that "you may not share your sports opinion while, at the same time, being a woman." DiCaro has firsthand experience as a recipient of gendered online harassment, having received threats and insults in response to her opinions on the investigation of a rape allegedly committed by hockey player Patrick Kane. The backlash DiCaro received was the impetus of the "#MoreThanMean" PSA, in which she collaborated with fellow sportscaster Sarah Spain. According to the PSA, these were among the tweets DiCaro received:

One of the players should beat you to death with a hockey stick like the whore you are, cunt.

This is why we don't hire any females unless we need our cocks sucked or our food cooked.

Hopefully this skank Julie DiCaro is Bill Cosby's next [rape] victim. That would be classic.

Even DiCaro's identity as a rape victim was used against her.

Why even bring up your own rape in this story? Is it your way of firing back at critics who said you can't get any?

I hope you get raped again. (Just Not Sports 2016)

These tweets were primarily sent by fans of the Chicago Blackhawks (DiCaro 2015)—the hockey club that employed Kane at the time of the investigation—in response to DiCaro's opinion that the player should have been placed on leave while his case was adjudicated, a suggestion that many viewed as a presumption of Kane's guilt. Therefore, the purpose of the tweets directed at DiCaro was not only to delegitimize her seemingly feminist opinion but also to degrade her enough to cause her to hesitate to offer her opinions again. While DiCaro has not stopped sharing her opinions about rape, sexual assault, and domestic violence in sports, the tweets culled for the PSA appeared to have achieved the desired effect of causing her emotional distress. At one point during the PSA, after one of the "average Joes" read a tweet directed at her, DiCaro visibly fought back tears despite knowing the tweet was going to be read. It can be surmised, then, that online harassment directed at women sportscasters in response to their (feminist) opinions serves not only to delegitimize their opinions but also to discipline them for speaking up.

Sexualization and Objectification

Sexualization and objectification is another form of online harassment that women sportscasters often endure. Social networking sites such as Twitter also serve as a site of sexualization and objectification, doing so in a way that, not unlike the appearance double standard, serves to diminish perceived female sportscaster credibility. More than the harassment women sportscasters endure in response to their opinions, this form of online harassment is greatly informed by gendered neoliberal, postfeminist discourse.

Samantha, the sports talk radio update anchor in her early twenties, told me that, on multiple occasions, she was mentioned by her station's listeners in tweets that were meant to sexualize and objectify her. First, she recalled an instance in which she tweeted about her new role with one of her station's popular programs. In response, according to Samantha, a sports media consumer tweeted, "Finally [Samantha's new] show has some eye candy. Too bad it's radio." She remembered not being as bothered by that tweet as the other two she recalled. Second, when her station sent a tweet promoting an upcoming on-air Twitter poll segment led by Samantha, someone responded by tweeting, "Forget the Twitter poll, can [Samantha] get on a [stripper] pole?" The third objectifying tweet Samantha recalled receiving, one in which someone suggested she would look better if she underwent lip injections, was the one that had the greatest emotional impact. "I was kind of upset by it for a little bit," she said. As referenced in chapter 1, Patricia recounted that many of her station's tweets that included photos promoting its all-women newscasts received responses that critiqued Patricia and her colleagues' bodies. In a blog post about Twitter, Sam Ponder (2013) recalled receiving a tweet in which someone suggested she opt for breast enhancement surgery.

This type of harassment, in which the bodies of women like Samantha and Ponder are critiqued and objectified, echo two postfeminist hallmarks: (self-)surveillance, which calls upon women to constantly monitor their femininity, and our culture's obsession and normalization of makeovers and cosmetic surgery (Gill 2007). As it relates to self-surveillance, these two sportscasters admitted to becoming conscious of their appearance—and, more specifically, their "flaws"—as a result of the messages they received from Twitter users. In this instance, in which cosmetic surgery was recommended to both women, postfeminism's, and therefore gendered neoliberalism's, constructions of femininity were brought to bear on Samantha and Ponder. Also, if we extrapolate the impact of such online interactions to woman sportscaster self-surveillance, it is not difficult to imagine sportscasters spending more time tending to certain cosmetic flaws, especially those related to hair, makeup, and clothing. When this happens, any such maintenance usually subscribes to ideal standards of Anglocentric femininity. Such maintenance therefore becomes another instance in which socially embedded norms influence sportscasting, gendering and racializing the industry. At the same time, such maintenance also contributes to the industry's gendering of society at large. In this case, the way women are visually represented when they appear on television or online further normalizes those socially embedded norms.

Of course, otherwise anonymous sports media consumers are not the only people who disseminate tweets that objectify and sexualize women sportscasters. Then–Chicago area sportscaster Aiyana Cristal was the target of objectification when a local sports talk radio host,

Dan Bernstein, tweeted, "I have no rooting interest in [Cristal's] work, but [I do] enjoy her giant boobs" (Feder 2015, para. 5). The focus on Cristal's breasts—as well as Samantha's lips and Ponder's bust—echoes the postfeminist hallmark of "femininity as a bodily property" and its attendant obsession with women's bodies (Gill 2007, 255), which essentially equates a woman's worth to her possession of a "sexy" body. Comments made by Boston sports talk radio host Kirk Minihane about Erin Andrews further demonstrates the way a woman sportscaster's worth correlates to her possession of a feminine body. In arguing that Andrews is not a good reporter, Minihane said, "I think if she weighed 15 more pounds, she'd be a waitress at Perkins" (Feitelberg 2014). In other words, Minihane believes Andrews's body alone makes her worthy of airtime.

Perhaps the most infamous instance of the online objectification and sexualization of a woman sportscaster came in November 2014. American comedian Artie Lange, a disciple of *The Howard Stern Show*, published a series of tweets to his more than 280,000 followers that described, in explicit detail, a sexual fantasy he imagined while watching then-host of ESPN's *First Take* Cari Champion one morning. The tweets about Champion, a Black woman, show that racism can be mixed with objectification:

> Here's the scenario I'm using to jerkoff to chick on First Take. I'm T[homas] Jefferson & she's my slave. She beats the shit out of me & runs free.

> I attempt to whip @CariChampion cuz she disrespected the Jefferson Plantation but she grabs whip & beats me. . . . I cum like a fat founding father (Duffy 2014).

Taken together, these objectifying and sexualizing internet comments remind women sportscasters—and sports media consumers—that a woman's ability as a sportscaster is of secondary importance to the presumed tastes of sports media consumers compared to their looks.

A Hybrid Form of Online Harassment

Just as the prioritization of appearance discursively diminishes the female sportscaster's perceived credibility, online objectification is also used to discredit women sportscasters who give their opinions, as happened to Lizzy and Sam Ponder. Gendered neoliberalism's entanglements and contradictions pervade this hybrid form of online harassment.

As referenced in chapter 1, images of ESPN commentator Sarah Spain donning the revealing clothing she wore early in her career are sometimes used by sports media consumers to weaken Spain's credibility as an outspoken feminist sports media personality. Spain often speaks publicly about violence against women and other issues related to gender inequality in the sports world. That she once wore revealing attire is often used to discredit these views, much in the same way a trial lawyer questions a witness's lifestyle as a means of discrediting their testimony. Immediately following and in response to the release of "#MoreThanMean," a Twitter account operated by the Chicago sports blog *SportsMockery* tweeted an image of Spain in a low-cut top along with the message, "Must be the public's fault her top is falling off, she obviously didn't mean for you to see [her cleavage]." Similarly, Sam Ponder's critique of the blogosphere, in the aftermath of the Ray Rice domestic violence incident, was also met with online backlash from *Barstool's* David Portnoy (2014, para. 3): Ponder "has a job because she's hot," he wrote. "It's requirement #1 for female sports reporters. They are hired to be objectified. . . . That's what you signed up for honey. Don't complain about it and play dumb after the fact." These responses mirror the objectification manifestation of online harassment and the appearance double standard's impact on perceived woman sportscaster credibility.

The attacks against Spain and Ponder are also couched in the gendered neoliberal entanglement between feminist and antifeminist discourses. Here, feminist discourses (calling out the prioritization of appearance and inequitable standards of dress for women in the industry) are co-opted to advance antifeminist ideas (in this case, repudiations of Spain and Ponder's claims of harassment and objectification of women sportscasters). The sophistication of this approach to discrediting women sportscasters through the entanglement of discourses ignores all nuance and therefore makes it challenging to advance the sort of feminist critiques Spain and Ponder disseminated on Twitter. This approach, which is a hallmark of the postfeminist, neoliberal moment, contributes to the construction of the neoliberal female sportscaster subjectivity by reinforcing notions of women's empowerment and choice. Without the benefit of nuance—in this case, the ability to explain that women are damned if they do and damned if they don't with respect to appearance—the ideal neoliberal female sportscaster subject reinforces the perception that the decisions she makes are empowered and freely chosen, even though the decisions she is confronted with have no desirable outcomes.

Popular Misogyny and the Funhouse Mirror

FOX Sports personality Clay Travis offered a similarly sophisticated response to a feminist media product that was especially relevant to women sportscasters, the "#MoreThanMean" public service announcement. Travis's response was rooted in gendered neoliberal discourse, specifically popular misogyny, which is a backlash to popular feminism, a highly visible, safe, "happy," and uncritical form of feminism (Banet-Weiser 2018). Popular misogyny not only repudiates popular feminism but also legitimizes the latter's necessity.

The 2016 release of the PSA cast a glaring light on the issue of gendered online harassment in general and that which targeted women in sports media in particular. To be sure, men sportscasters and other public figures face online harassment as well, but not simply because they are men; unlike women, their gender is not used by online harassers to make them feel or appear inferior. As Soraya Chemaly (2014, para. 7), director of the Women's Media Center Speech Project, wrote, "For girls and women, [online] harassment is not just about 'unpleasantries.' It's often about men asserting dominance, silencing, and frequently, scaring and punishing them." The difference between hurling insults at a man and using a woman's gender to police her behavior and attitudes is the crux of the meaning behind the title of "#MoreThanMean." That is, the PSA attempts to demonstrate that the gendered online harassment of women in sports media, and in society at large, are more than "mean" comments that are simply meant to insult someone.

Nevertheless, FOX Sports personality Clay Travis took to Twitter to criticize the PSA for highlighting an issue that he believes is not unique to women. "I'm confident that my mentions are tougher than

99.9% of all people, male or female, receive on Twitter," he tweeted (Travis 2016c), before adding that he and his children have had their lives threatened on Twitter (Travis 2016b). Travis was not alone in his dissent. His FOX Sports and *Outkick* colleague Jason Whitlock (2016a) added that "Twitter isn't remotely a safe space. Everyone who states an opinion from an elevated platform gets mean tweets." This reaction to the PSA, like gendered online harassment itself, is a manifestation of popular misogyny, a backlash against popular feminism, rooted in the idea that women are afforded an "unfair protectionism" (Banet-Weiser 2018, 62). Due to an assumption of a level playing field between men and women, mediated products such as "#MoreThan-Mean" are viewed, through the lens of popular misogyny, as part of a "series of repeated injuries" against (white) men. Indeed, Whitlock (2016b) described the PSA as being part of a "public relations campaign for Social Justice Warriors."

Travis took his popular misogynistic rhetoric a step further. Travis (2016a) added to his response to the PSA by tweeting a link to a video and described it by writing, "Here's my mom . . . reading a few of the mean tweets sent to me. Her accent makes these great." While the video was originally produced and disseminated a year before "#MoreThan-Mean" (FOX Sports 2015), Travis redistributed it within the context of his response to the PSA. His video therefore exemplified popular misogyny's funhouse mirroring effect (Banet-Weiser 2018, 63). The effect is so called because this approach to misogynistic critique, much like a funhouse at a carnival, often "mirrors" the speech it attempts to delegitimize while distorting that speech to serve misogyny. This approach is effective because mirroring recognizes and harnesses "the power of the visual" and is therefore central to an economy of visibility that is nurtured by our neoliberal culture (62). Banet-Weiser uses the mirrored yet distorted response to the declaration that Black Lives Matter—which states that *all* lives matter—as an example of the funhouse mirror effect, showing that it can also be used to perpetuate racism. In an economy of visibility, an economy in which individuals and social movements both participate, the decision to have "#MoreThan-Mean" mirror the "mean tweets" segment on Jimmy Kimmel's late-night talk show was strategic: the PSA mirrored a familiar and highly visible format in an attempt to advance feminist discourse.

Travis's decision to redistribute his video, amid the discussion of "#MoreThanMean," was similarly strategic within this economy of visibility. However, while Travis used the video to argue that online harassment is not unique to women sports journalists, to some, the tone of his video—and of his tweet reintroducing it—undermined his argument. As Sean Newell (2016, para. 8) wrote for *Vice*, "Note the vibe in each of the videos. . . . Try to process the difference between when [Liz Travis] laughs because she just said 'shit' and when a dude apologizes to DiCaro for reading something to her he didn't even write." Travis's video and his tweet reintroducing it are meant to treat the subject as lighthearted and humorous. Even the blog post in which Travis (2015b, para. 4) first introduced the video presented the segment as a form of entertainment while ignoring the gravity of the subject of online harassment: "So what's it sound like when a Southern grandma of six reads some of the worst things people say to me online? It's glorious."

Additionally, Travis's response ignores the context of the tweets he receives and how that context differs from those received by women working in sports media. "There is an ocean of difference between being unilaterally attacked for doing a job, which is what the #MoreThanMean video is about, and people engaging you when you are actively trying to get a rise out of them" (Newell 2016, para. 8). Travis is known for antagonizing the political left in the United States, famously arguing, for example, that there was no basis for the protests against racism at the University of Missouri (Travis 2015a), despite evidence to the contrary (Seltzer 2018). To be clear, there is no excuse for threatening someone with violence online, regardless of their political leanings or gender.

However, Travis's argument against "#MoreThanMean" ignores several important nuances: the fact that, by his own admission, "like a pig who loves wallowing in the slop, [he] can't get enough of the [online] hate" (Travis 2015b, para. 1); the fact that, because he is a white man with a law degree and possesses the advantages and privileges that come with that social location, he can more comfortably wallow in his own "slop" than a woman can; and the fact that women are disproportionately the targets of online harassment. Indeed, 70 percent of all online harassment is directed at women, with women of color receiving more (Citron 2014, as cited in Banet-Weiser 2018).

Treating harassment as comedic entertainment while ignoring the nuances of gendered mistreatment, as Travis does in reintroducing his video, is central to the funhouse mirror effect. It "contorts and distorts the realities of systemic sexism so that this reality somehow works in favor of popular misogyny" (Banet-Weiser 2018, 61). These distortions are often in the form of parody, which serves to distract us and "direct our attention elsewhere, belittling the problem itself." The use of humor and irony as a means of expressing sexist views is also central to postfeminist discourse; if sexist speech is humorous, the person delivering the humor can disavow his or her sexism by passing it off as it a joke (Gill 2007). Given these intersecting gendered neoliberal discourses, Travis's approach to addressing "#MoreThanMean"—sharing what was meant to be a humorous and entertaining video that mirrors the PSA—is a tried and true staple of misogynistic discourse in the contemporary, neoliberal moment. By equating the online harassment of white male antagonists to that targeting women sports reporters and by using humor to distract from the issue and the material impact it has on women working in sports media, online harassment is delegitimized as an issue the sports media industry must address. Instead, it becomes just another issue neoliberal women sportscasters are asked to overcome. After all, the logic goes, if male sports media figures can do it, and even relish it, so can women in the industry. Furthermore, in the absence of meaningful institutional assistance in navigating online harassment and as the foundation of the discourse that informs such harassment, gendered neoliberalism legitimizes its necessity for those women who wish to enter and thrive in the industry.

Conclusion

Like Western women in other industries, women in sportscasting are forced to endure online and offline gendered harassment. These manifestations of harassment doubly contribute to the construction of the neoliberal female sportscaster subjectivity. First, the many forms of such harassment are informed to varying degrees by gendered neoliberal discourse. Gendered neoliberalism's entanglements and contradictions inform the female sportscaster's reproductive paradox as well as her objectification online. Gendered neoliberalism also informs the double standards and bias that buttress quid pro quo and stalking as well as the popular misogyny that repudiates any feminist critique offered by women sportscasters. Secondly, the affective (or emotional) impact of harassment—not just the harassment itself—further causes women sportscasters to employ neoliberal logic in order to enter and survive the industry.

In chapter 4, I turn to the affective labor prompted by harassment and its relationship with gendered neoliberalism and the female sportscaster subjectivity. The sportscasting industry's dependence on neoliberal discourses dictates that women in the industry are expected to manage their emotions in the face of harassment, with little to no meaningful assistance. This expectation normalizes the harassment described previously and, as a result, broadly absolves the industry of any responsibility for the harassment its women endure.

FOUR

The Woman Sportscaster's Affective Labor

Sara Ahmed (2014, 12) writes in *The Cultural Politics of Emotion* that "emotions show us how power shapes the very surface of bodies as well as worlds." Women sportscasters' emotions in response to double standards, bias, and harassment occupy a pivotal role in shaping the body of the neoliberal female sportscaster as well as the world of sportscasting. Ahmed's volume has become a foundational text in an emerging field in cultural studies known as affect—with an *a* sound similar to that in the word *acting*—which seeks to investigate the way emotions impact individuals, institutions, and society at large. Affect theory is utilized under the notion that "emotions should not be regarded as psychological states, but as social and cultural practices" (Ahmed 2014, 9). That is, emotions are not simply involuntary reactions to psychological or even physical stimuli. Instead, emotions are a performance, insofar as we as a collective people have learned to "control emotions, and to experience the 'appropriate' emotions at different times and places" (Elias 1978, as cited in Ahmed 2014, 3). In this case, women sportscasters have had to learn to control their emotions in accordance with the demands of an industry whose primary mechanism for constructing and maintaining its gendered structure is neoliberalism. Sportscasting, as with many other institutions, is a site in which "some emotions are 'elevated' as signs of [an individual's sophistication], whilst others remain 'lower' as signs of weakness" (Ahmed 2014, 3). In that vein, women sportscasters are taught that emotions that may be "appropriate" responses to gendered mistreatment in other contexts are viewed as "signs of weakness" in sportscasting.

Ahmed's work calls upon a group of scholars who have previously studied the sociocultural implications of emotions, including Arlie Hochschild. Hochschild (1979, 552) drew distinctions between two approaches to studying emotive experiences: the first examines the social factors that cause us to exhibit certain emotions and the second investigates the way social factors make us think and feel about, assess, and manage our emotions. The latter approach, "emotion management," was crucial to Hochschild's work and is also vital to this chapter. While previous chapters established double standards and harassment as the foremost practices that evoke "negative" woman sportscaster emotions, this chapter serves as an analysis of the impact those practices have on the way women sportscasters assess and manage their emotions and how that assessment and management of emotions contributes to the construction of the neoliberal female sportscaster subjectivity. In addition, this chapter offers an analysis of the impact this affective labor has on the gendered structure of the sportscasting industry overall.

I have argued elsewhere that scholarship that "takes affect under consideration is of great import if sports media [scholars and practitioners] are to achieve greater quantitative and representational equality for women," (Harrison 2018, 254). To study the impact of affect on women sportscasters is to provide "a critique of a model of social structure that neglects the emotional intensities, which allow such structures to be reified as forms of being" (Ahmed 2014, 12). Stated another way, sportscasting as an institution continually ignores affect as it pertains to women sportscasters and therefore perpetuates the subordination of women in the industry. If we start by acknowledging that women sportscasters endure double standards, bias, and harassment, what are the long-term individual and institutional effects of the effort required to navigate those phenomena? An analysis of what Hochschild (1979, 562) calls the "secondary acts" that ensue after emotive experiences is one such attempt at using an affective approach to answer this question.

When viewed through the lens of Hochschild's emotion management, the ability to manage one's emotions is a skill women sportscasters have been forced to exhibit in both professional and private contexts to gain entrée into and thrive within the sportscasting industry. Again, the pervasiveness of gendered double standards, bias, and harassment is not unique to sportscasting; women the world over have grown accustomed to managing their emotions in and out of the workplace. As I have written in this volume's first three chapters, many women and men within the sportscasting industry even recognize that these forms of gendered mistreatment exist. Nevertheless, in accordance with the contemporary moment, the industry continues to depend on neoliberalism as a compass for women to navigate that gendered mistreatment. As a result, women sportscasters must manage and discipline their emotions with little to no meaningful institutional help. This process of managing emotions, I argue, is the cornerstone of the neoliberal female sportscaster subjectivity. Without the ability to mind one's emotions in a way the industry deems suitable, the female sportscaster cannot possibly overcome double standards, bias, or harassment. This chapter is an analysis of that process and how it is brought to bear on the female sportscaster subjectivity, the material experiences of women sportscasters, and the gendered structure of the industry as a whole.

With respect to emotion management, Hochschild's work distinguishes two types: emotional labor and emotion work, both of which form the basis of the arguments advanced in this chapter. Within the context of the sportscasting industry, Hochschild's (1983) concept of *emotional labor*—which is performed in the workplace in exchange for wages—can be expanded to include a form of work that is undertaken by women in the industry seeking to gain social capital. The necessity of emotional labor is evident in women sportscasters' sentiment that women in the industry require "thick skin" in response to bias and harassment. Additionally, the *emotion work* (Hochschild 1979) required of women sportscasters contributes to the gendered structure of the sportscasting industry (and sports in general) by calling upon women to accept outside of the workplace patronizing support and assistance from managers, colleagues, family members, and friends who all take double standards, bias, and harassment for granted. Since the industry has failed to adequately address these issues, they have been normalized as obstacles that (ideal, neoliberal) women sportscasters should expect to endure. As it pertains to the gendered structure of the industry, this expectation also has the consequence of deterring some women from entering or staying in sportscasting, thus ensuring that the industry quantitatively and qualitatively remains a male-dominated industry.

Emotional Labor, Thick Skin, and Trolls

Emotional labor is employed primarily in customer service industries such as tourism and hospitality and has exchange value insofar as an employee can earn a wage in exchange for it (Hochschild 1983, 8). In such service industries, employees are asked to follow "display rules" or guidelines that dictate how workers are expected to act in face-to-face or voice-to-voice interactions with customers (Ekman 1992). In general, emotional laborers are expected to provide "friendly" customer service that is manifest as a "publicly observable facial and bodily display" (8), regardless of their own personal feelings with regard to the task at hand. Sportscasters are not customer service agents per se—the commodity they exchange is information, not "service with a smile," nor do they earn a wage in direct exchange for their ability to provide friendly service or conform to display rules. Nevertheless, part of a woman sportscaster's job is to follow a set of display rules despite personal or professional turmoil, such as that endured by Sara Walsh, who went on the air while bleeding from a miscarriage. Emotional labor within this professional setting therefore serves as a currency with which women sportscasters accrue social capital that can be used to gain the influence and favor necessary to enter and thrive in the industry. Given the gender wage gap, one may even argue that this social capital may also serve as a substitute for actual, monetary compensation commensurate with what male sportscasters receive.

I define social capital in a workplace context as an intangible asset one accrues to varying degrees that allows that person to influence relationships with (and decision-making by) others. To be sure, women sportscasters are not decision-makers per se; they do not generally have much say in hiring decisions, for example. Instead, the sort of influence I believe women in on-air positions in the industry accumulate is the kind of influence that allows them to be hired, retained, and promoted. That is, there appears to be a prevailing assumption that a woman sportscaster who does not accrue social capital through emotional labor can find it difficult to navigate the industry, particularly early in one's career. As neoliberalism places the onus on individuals for their own economic success and upward mobility despite various forms of oppression, and emotional labor is an on-the-job mechanism through which women can achieve that success, an adherence to neoliberalism has become an unwritten yet essential duty performed by women sportscasters.

This process of gaining social capital through emotional labor was evident in the case of Marie. In her first job out of college, as described in chapter 3, Marie endured hostile work environment sexual harassment from a sports director who not only cornered her in her station's small audio booth but also thought it necessary to know when Marie would menstruate. "I was terrified," she said, "but I didn't really say anything to [the station's executives] at that moment because I had just gotten the job and I felt like I couldn't say anything. I didn't want to have their attention right from the start." Although the harassment Marie endured evoked a feeling of terror, she could not display that emotion to her superiors because of the lack of social capital she had accrued at her station.

Emotional labor is also manifest in the belief that, as many of the women I interviewed expressed, women sportscasters must have thick skin. In all instances, "thick skin" was used to describe the temperament a woman sportscaster must present in the face of gendered criticism and mistreatment. A central component of one's temperament is the emotions they display. Thus, the act of developing a thick skin is a form of emotional labor. Women sportscasters believe that to enter and thrive in the industry, they must develop the ability to display a calm, unaffected temperament when facing gendered mistreatment.

While both men and women in on-air positions often speak of the need for thick skin, the thick skins they respectively develop make them seemingly impervious to different forms of critique. A man sportscaster might endure harsh and even insulting criticism for a poor performance. In such a case, the man sportscaster's gender, a key component of his identity, is not usually used to belittle or dehumanize him. In response to criticism of a poor performance, a male sportscaster can alter or improve his performance after enduring harsh criticism. On the other hand, a woman sportscaster often endures criticism and mistreatment that is rooted in (hetero)sexism; she can alter her performance, but she is still a woman. The distinction between the respective purposes of male and female sportscasters' thick skin represents another inequitable obstacle women in sportscasting often grapple with.

Amelia spoke about what she perceived to be the importance of developing thick skin as she discussed the negative attention she has seen other women sportscasters receive simply for being women. Mistreatment "can leave a mark, right? So, then, you would not feel confident . . . but I think you also have to have thick skin." Amelia then recounted times, early in her career, in which male athletes she covered gave her skeptical looks in responses to questions she asked, simply because she, a woman, was the one asking the questions. In her mind, women reporters who aspire to successful careers—however those are defined—have no choice but to maintain a positive attitude despite such interactions. According to Amelia, "For the women out there that go in with a negative attitude about it—[those interactions] can be damning."

While Amelia might seem dismissive of the gendered mistreatment women sportscasters endure, her comments are emblematic of the active management of one's emotions when faced with gendered mistreatment. The accrual of social workplace capital is a motivating factor in the woman sportscaster's active performance of—and compliance with—emotional labor. Moreover, it appears this performance serves as a form of cognitive emotion work, in which women sportscasters manage their thoughts as a way of altering the emotions they display (Hochschild 1979). The phrase "fake it 'til you make it" applies here; in theory, if a woman sportscaster can actively feign an unaffected disposition, it becomes easier to actually be unaffected. ESPN's Michelle Beadle echoed this sentiment in a profile of her in *Hollywood Reporter* (2013, para. 10): "It's definitely a business where if you're self-conscious at all, you either grow a thick skin or at least fake like you have one." Once a woman sportscaster does the work of dissociating herself from her feelings, it becomes easier to accrue the sort of social capital she needs to thrive and advance in the industry. In an increasingly neoliberal society, women sportscasters must therefore take it upon themselves to be resourceful and resilient in their response to gendered mistreatment. The expectation that women need to be enterprising in this case is part and parcel of the construction of the neoliberal female sportscaster subjectivity.

Instead of displaying the emotions that harassment and the like typically evoke, women in the sportscasting industry have accepted the idea that the best way to subvert workplace mistreatment is to actively display emotions that are not actually felt. One such strategy often employed by the women I interviewed is the use of humor. "I used humor as a deflection," said Nancy, the hall-of-famer. "That was my thing. That's how I got through it." Hannah took a similar tack earlier in her career. As a reporter, whenever she expressed an interest in expanding her skills by attempting the anchor role, her general manager would discourage her from doing so by using language she deemed "very inappropriate." Although she admitted wanting to respond by saying, "Don't talk to me that way," Hannah concluded that it was more appropriate to display an unaffected disposition. "So, it's one of those things, where I just suck it up and smile and laugh it off, pretty much." Both Nancy and Hannah have endured workplace interactions that left them feeling insulted or humiliated and have found that the best way to display thick skin is by laughing at the insulting or humiliating comments. This strategy has become increasingly expected as sexism in the neoliberal moment is often framed in "irony and knowingness," blurring the lines between what is sexist and what is meant to be humorous or satirical (Gill 2007, 266).

But what happens when sexism is obvious and is purposely hurtful, such as the sort of comments directed at Julie DiCaro in the "#MoreThanMean" PSA? Given the increasing expectation that women sportscasters interact with their audience online—and the harassment women endure there—women in the industry have had to be strategic about the way they manage their emotions in the social media environment. Some women sports journalists have described that strategy as "troll management" (Everbach 2018). In that vein, Jane shared the same sentiments expressed by Nancy and Amelia: an unaffected disposition is required for women sportscasters, even in response to online harassment that is purposely hurtful. "You have to have thick skin in this business," Jane said, echoing the ubiquitous refrain, which preceded an even more revealing comment: "You have to think that— and people shared this with me in the industry—[it] just tends to be the people who fire back the fastest or whatnot are the ones who literally just sit on their couch all day, and they get pleasure in being rude and harsh and whatever it is, attacking, bullying you, and you have to let it slide." Jane, in consultation with others within the industry, believes that an effective way of dealing with online harassers is to imagine them as trolls who find joy in emotionally harming others. In theory, this approach helps women sportscasters to understand the purpose of the harassment and makes it easier to (pretend to) ignore. This approach is an example of cognitive emotion work; by changing the image she has of her harassers, Jane hopes to change the emotions she feels when she encounters them.

According to Patricia, however, the strategy of ignoring her harassers is easier said than done. "Sometimes you get really down on yourself when people write in just absolutely trashing you," she said before noting that the harshest and most unjust criticism she receives is related to her appearance and not her performance. Ultimately, however, Patricia is quite familiar with emotional labor. She used variations of the phrase "have to have a thick skin" three times when discussing her experiences. She did not use the phrase passively. When discussing the viewers who endlessly comment on her appearance, for example, Patricia admitted using a similar approach to the one detailed by Jane: "And it's from people who I know have nothing else better to do than to sit at home and just hate everything they see—and unfortunately there are a bunch of miserable human beings out there. So, it's just kind of like I have to put it out of my mind and have a thick skin about it." In other words, because her harassers behave in this manner, she feels obligated to manage her emotions—in a Hochschildian sense—by reframing her harassers as trolls, making it easier for her to ignore them. Later in her interview, Patricia implied that her harassers are not trolls but human beings engaging in antisocial behavior that compels her to manage her emotions. "We shouldn't have to have thick skin. People should know better than to comment on those things. But it is what it is."

While Patricia did not use the terms *emotional labor* or *performance* to describe her approach to contending with online harassment, she is aware—as were Nancy, Hannah, Michelle Beadle, and Jane—that she is tasked with a performance, one that requires her to intentionally display feelings that differ from those she actually feels. Like the four women referenced, Patricia has implicitly accepted emotional labor as a compulsory part of her job. To not do so would risk her social capital and her emotional relationship with her career. After investing so much time and resources in training to be a sportscaster, Patricia and her peers have much to lose if they do not come to enjoy their jobs. This feeling of enjoyment would be difficult to achieve if negative feelings were evoked and displayed with each instance of harassment or mistreatment. The desire to thrive in and enjoy one's career thus appears to be another motivating factor in the acceptance of emotional labor.

Many service workers (e.g., customer service representatives, flight attendants, and restaurant servers) also encounter emotional labor as an essential job duty. However, unlike women sportscasters, service workers are trained by their employers—many of whom have elaborate customer service training modules—to handle upset and unruly guests after they obtain jobs that call for the maintenance of a demeanor that is at once calm, friendly, and hospitable. Conversely, most women sportscasters acquire their journalistic skills through college training and, in many cases, internships. As of this writing, I am not aware of a collegiate program that prepares future or new sports journalists for the emotional labor they need to perform when entering the workforce, particularly in response to online harassment (except by fostering an environment in which those student journalists may be forced to undergo neoliberal emotional labor while in college!). Such a training would seem more important now than ever, given the growing expectation that sportscasters actively maintain an online presence. Many colleges have chapters of the Association of Women in Sports Media, through which aspiring women sports journalists can commiserate with peers and industry professionals about the challenges women encounter in the industry. Similarly, FOX Sports sideline reporter Laura Okmin manages an organization called GALvanize, which not only teaches women how to be better sportscasters but also how to deal with the challenges afflicting women in the industry. Though these organizations provide affective labor training of some sort, they are typically not mandated as part of any college curriculum. Furthermore, and most importantly, in the absence of meaningful structural change enacted by the sportscasting industry, the Association of Women in Sports Media and GALvanize essentially prepare students for lives as neoliberal female sports journalists.

Even if there was such curricular training widely available in journalism programs, there still would be no such preparation for the students who do not pursue journalism as course of study. Paula, for example, was not a journalism student in college and admitted to being surprised when she entered the industry, to the extent that she "didn't know what I was getting myself into. I didn't realize how tough a skin I needed to [have] in the business, to be honest." In truth, even if colleges and media organizations undertook emotional labor training of some kind, it likely would not be as effective or as applicable as that which service industry employers offer, which can be more general in such training. Unlike women in most service industries, women sportscasters have their work and likenesses distributed to wide audiences and archived in perpetuity. This distribution and archiving allows for repetitive gendered mistreatment by way of references by many social media users to previous work and appearances, as was the case for Sarah Spain.

Samantha is also familiar with the affective labor women are required to perform in the online environment. In one instance, reacting to an online comment that she "belonged in the kitchen," Samantha took the familiar approach of cognitively reframing her harasser as a troll. "For all I know," she said, "you're a girl that's jealous or a guy in your mom's basement. So, I try really hard [not to let comments like that affect me] and that one didn't bother me." Nevertheless, it is no simple task for Samantha to display an unaffected disposition in the face of negative comments made about her online, something she admitted a few moments later. "I try not to let those things bother me, and some days I'm better at it than others." The implication here is that she has received comments that *have* bothered her, such as the suggestion related in chapter 3 that she should undergo lip injections. When comments like that are made, she says, "I never let it upset my [ability to do my] job or let anyone know it's bothering me [but] for a while my confidence was not very good [after that comment]."

After the lip injection comment, instead of cognitively reframing her harasser and feigning indifference, Samantha admitted that she was upset. To cope with the interaction and to help manage her emotions, she sought the assistance of a relative. This approach exemplifies Hochschild's emotion-work system, a significant component of her conceptualization of emotion management and one that is often used by women sportscasters to navigate gendered neoliberal expectations.

Emotion Work and Patronizing Support

As women sportscasters are humans who live lives outside the workplace, they often reflect on the day's events outside the work setting and assess the emotions they exhibited as a result of those events. Thus, the female sportscaster's neoliberal work of managing her emotions does not simply cease when she leaves the studio, stadium, or arena or when she logs off social media (which many men are accustomed to suggesting). The process of reflecting and assessing one's emotions *after* certain interactions is what Hochschild (1979, 562) calls "emotion work." When people perform emotion work, they often confide in others—friends, family, and coworkers who together form an "emotion-work system"—as they assess their emotional responses to the day's experiences. The emotion-work system's status as an optional emotion management strategy shows that emotion work can either be a communal practice or a solitary one. In either case, people who undergo emotion work often reach a moment that Hochschild calls a "pinch," a moment of cognitive dissonance in which people assess their emotional displays as having been incongruous to the situation in which the emotions were felt. This dissonance, according to Hochschild, is usually determined by the emotions the person wishes to feel or believes are more appropriate to feel.

Emotion work, like emotional labor, is commonplace for women in the male-dominated sportscasting industry. The "pinch" for women sportscasters typically occurs immediately after cases of harassment or unfair treatment. In these instances, the feelings that often ensue neither match those that the woman sportscaster wants to feel (happy, confident, or empowered) nor what she believes she is permitted to feel or exhibit, lest her emotions be perceived as a sign of weakness or as those of a "difficult" employee or colleague. This additional emotion work—and affective labor more broadly—can have the effect of driving some women away from the industry. Ironically, this attrition legitimizes gendered neoliberalism since those women who choose not to conform to its principles and perform the necessary emotion work are those women who "can't hack it."

After receiving the suggestion that she consider lip injections, Samantha sought the comfort of her mother to help her work through an emotion-work pinch. The sports talk radio update anchor was insulted by the suggestion yet wanted to feel—and thought it more appropriate to feel, for the sake of her relationship with her job—unaffected by the comment. "And I was kind of upset by it for a little bit, but my mom was like, 'Why? You're letting someone that's never seen you in person [determine] what you think about yourself.' . . . But then I [realized], like, yeah, you're right, they haven't seen me in person, so why do I care?" On the surface, and certainly in Samantha's case, it appears that emotion-work systems can be a healthy outlet for working through one's emotions, especially if one has gotten in the habit of compartmentalizing them.

Emotion-work systems typically contribute to gendered neoliberalism, however, by normalizing gendered mistreatment and offering solutions rooted in neoliberal logic. Lizzy related to me in chapter 1 her experience as a young woman whose qualifications for a previous job were questioned because of a perception that she earned her position by sleeping with athletes. "I could deal with the 'You only got your job because you're pretty,'" she said. "I could deal with the 'You only got your job because you're a girl.' But when they attacked my character, that really upset me." Lizzy later called this a "trying moment" that made her question her desire to work in sports media. Soon after hearing that comment, Lizzy recalled retreating to her car, crying, and calling her father, who gave her what she described as a "harsh reality talk." After telling Lizzy that she should not be upset because the assumption she had slept with athletes was not true, her father added, "'This isn't going to get any easier for you.' You know, 'This is going to happen to you if you choose to go down this path of sports media.'" Lizzy's father told her that she needed to be confident in her abilities and ignore her doubters before adding, "'But you can't let them see you cry and you can't let them see you get upset because then they know that they've gotten to you.'" Her father's message normalized double standards, harassment, and neoliberal affective labor all in the span of a few sentences, which is not uncommon in woman sportscaster emotion-work systems. It is generally taken for granted that women in the sportscasting industry must endure harassment and other forms of gendered mistreatment, but messages like the one Lizzy received—that she ought to expect mistreatment and display an unaffected attitude—further legitimize gendered neoliberalism while also normalizing the subordination of women in the industry.

Just like the diminished perceived credibility of women sportscasters discussed in chapter 1, the assumption that women sportscasters should expect harassment is another instance in which a notion has become common sense, even though no group of people (e.g., men) intentionally sought to normalize this idea. Although power, in the Foucauldian sense, can marginalize certain groups of people, it is neither exercised by a single being or group nor always employed intentionally. Just as men did not collectively and actively decide to impose a double standard of appearance so as to weaken woman sportscaster credibility, men did not collectively issue a decree that instructs all people to view gendered double standards and harassment—and the emotion work that they necessitate—as normal. Instead, this knowledge was constructed through everyday discourse, over a lengthy period of time. However, as power is fluid, it is possible, albeit through a concerted, longtime effort, to modify perceptions of what is normal. So long as women sportscasters (and men, for that matter) are advised to accept and ignore mistreatment, cultural and structural change is unlikely to happen.

Consider the case of Sam Ponder (2013) who wrote a blog post about the first time she used Twitter professionally. Similar to Samantha's experience, a Twitter user suggested Ponder undergo cosmetic surgery to augment her breasts. After her initial reaction to the tweets, she confided in her emotion-work system. Her family gave her the usual encouragement: a directive from her father to "consider the source" (para. 15) and a suggestion to view her harassers as trolls. Ponder also enlisted the advice of Aaron Taylor, a former professional football player and sportscaster with whom Ponder had previously worked. His response was not a suggestion as much as it was a philosophical reading of the situation. In his view, "people can only hurt your feelings in areas you're already insecure. Does a tall guy care if someone calls him short?" (para. 17). Although Taylor's comment was well meaning on the surface, it also implicitly endorsed the gendered mistreatment of women sportscasters. He seemed to suggest that Ponder needed to employ emotion work to project an unaffected demeanor. To do otherwise, then, would be to imply that the comment was true, which would encourage more comments. And that's saying nothing of the fact that Ponder very well could have been insecure about her bust, rendering his philosophy moot, by his own logic. Regardless, Taylor's comment—like that made by Lizzy's father—placed the onus on Ponder for overcoming the harassment rather than on the person who made the suggestion.

Patricia received a much different response from a male colleague after she shared with him some comments she received online. Her colleague acknowledged that the behavior that compels people to harass women sportscasters online is not normal. "He just was like, 'I am so sorry that you have to deal with this shit constantly because it's so unacceptable that people think that it's perfectly fine.'" However, in the absence of consistent emotional support given—and institutional action taken—through this lens, women sportscasters must perform on their own the tasks of regulating their emotions and negotiating the compartmentalization the job presently requires. Coming to grips with this reality is therefore critical to the success of the neoliberal female sportscaster subject.

Unfortunately, as gendered neoliberalism has become de rigueur for women in the west, those who fail to conform to it also unwittingly legitimize its existence. That is, when a woman sportscaster chooses not to manage her emotions, she can be dismissed as having not been "tough" enough or resourceful enough or not having the right temperament to navigate the industry's obstacles for women. Marking women this way allows the industry to be more resolute in its assumption that women sportscasters need to have thick skin, even though it is more accurate to say that the industry has ignored the challenges that cause women to have to manage their emotions in the first place. While emotion management serves as an expedient solution that allows women sportscasters to navigate the industry in the present moment, it would be naïve to ignore the possibility that this increasingly essential job function might make the job less desirable for women, reinforcing sportscasting's marginalization of women.

Affective Labor and Marginalization

In an article written for *The Athletic*, Lisa Olson (2017)—who, in the early 1990s, was reassigned from her job at the *Boston Herald* to one in Australia after an instance of locker room harassment—introduces an adage that is, as Olson describes it, implicitly taught to "every female" who enters the sports media industry: "Check your dignity at the door" (para. 3). If women in the industry are willing to accept that they can never display their true feelings (to peers, consumers, and, to a lesser extent, themselves) after experiencing gendered mistreatment, they may find that they can enjoy successful careers in the business. "Forget your dignity, keep your head down and you'll get along fine," Olson writes. "If you're extremely lucky you might even go an entire season without an incident that demeans or belittles you, makes you feel as if you barely exist." Affective labor broadly, and emotion management more specifically, not only serve as tools that aid women sportscasters' efforts to "check their dignity at the door," but they have also become another essential job function, one that, for women sportscasters, ought to be included in their contracts, right before "other duties as assigned." It becomes easy, then, to imagine an instance in which the added burden of emotion management might be too much for one person to bear.

It becomes easier still to imagine an earlier "breaking point" for those women sportscasters who are non-white, non-cisgender, or non-heterosexual, are parents, or are away from home for the very first time. Paula, a Latina native of a coastal region, very nearly reached that point early in her career. Her first five and a half years in the business took her to white, rural, predominantly conservative markets that were far from home. One day, she received what she thought was her first fan letter. Instead, it was hate mail that asked her, among other things, to "do us all a favor and get the hell off our television screen." According to Paula, letters and emails like this were regular occurrences throughout the first five years of her career before she moved to a market closer to an urban center. Given the demographics of her early-career markets, the fact that she was the only woman sportscaster of color in those markets, and the fact that viewers often yearned in their correspondence with her to see more of—as she describes him—her less accomplished, monotone, "cookie-cutter" white male colleague, Paula chalked up the seemingly endless wave of disapproval to race *and* gender equally. Considering the Anglocentric expectations of woman sportscaster beauty and comportment described in chapter 1, this is a reasonable conclusion. None of the criticism Paula endured made as much of an emotional impact as that first letter, however. "Getting that piece of mail, it broke me," she said. "And the fact that it was continuously happening for five straight years was really heartbreaking, and really hard for me not to start believing what they said." Although Paula persisted and has no qualms about her career choice now, she said she nearly left the industry during those first five years.

We most often hear about the women who, like Paula, were the quintessential neoliberal women sportscasters who used emotion management to persevere and find a comfortable niche within the industry. With few exceptions (Everbach 2018), however, we rarely hear from those who voluntarily leave the industry or from those who, like Stephanie, hesitate to pursue a full-fledged career as sportscasters because of, among other expectations, the burden of emotion management placed on women sportscasters. Although Stephanie admitted that much of her hesitancy stems from the fact that she has already put her day job at risk by podcasting, she also stated that she would be more likely to want to become a full-time sportscaster "if it didn't come with all that baggage." Stephanie expressed a belief that a career as a baseball sportscaster would be fun "if somebody was just going to pay me to sit in front of a camera and talk about baseball all the time . . . but it's not quite enough for me for all the crap that comes with it." In Stephanie's view, emotion management is an essential job duty that cannot be divorced from a woman sportscaster's job.

The story of Lisa Guerrero, former *Monday Night Football* sideline reporter and current investigative reporter for *Inside Edition*, offers an example of a woman sportscaster who voluntarily left the industry in part because the emotion management the job required outweighed its benefits. In Lisa Olson's (2017) article for *The Athletic*, Guerrero told the story of the time she was humiliated at FOX Sports' roast of sports media personality and former Major League Baseball player John Kruk. Sitting on stage with her colleagues from FOX Sports' *The*

Best Damn Sports Show Period, Guerrero quickly became the target of the roast, enduring humiliating cracks about her breasts and jokes that she was able to land elusive interviews with men athletes by sleeping with them. Guerrero told Olson (2017, para. 43) that, after being brought to tears during the event, "I was so thrown and shaken from that John Kruk roast, it nearly broke me. After *Monday Night Football*, I went into a hole for a year. It completely flipped the script for me [as to] how I felt about myself and my value as a reporter."

Although most women in sports media are implicitly (and sometimes explicitly) told to check their dignity at the door, overcoming this episode required too much of Guerrero's dignity. While it is difficult to imagine that anything would amount to fair recompense for her humiliating experience, Guerrero was powerless to seek restitution. As Olson (2017, para. 42) wrote, "Women who complained were [viewed as] women who didn't belong in [the] business." Although she never explicitly stated in the article that the Kruk roast caused her to leave the industry, Guerrero (2017) tweeted a link to the article when it was published, along with a message that read: "Lots of people thru the years have asked me why I left sports broadcasting. In this wonderful article . . . I finally share one of the many reasons why."

The woman sportscaster emotion management stemming from harassment and gender inequality contributes to an institutional structure in which women are left on the periphery. The choice for women who are either in or considering entering the industry is clear: accept the status quo—in which women in the industry are humiliated, harassed, belittled, or otherwise subordinated—leave, or do not enter. No matter what a woman chooses, these options all reinforce men's predominance in sports media. Generally speaking, male sportscasters are not sexually harassed or belittled due to their gender. Because of this, they are less likely to want to leave the industry while gainfully employed. Similarly, because male sportscasters do not endure the same challenges that women sportscasters do, men are less likely to have to weigh the potential loss of their dignity—or the emotion management the job requires—against their desire to enter the field. All else being equal, this reality makes men more likely than women to attempt to embark on and tough out careers as sportscasters. In sum, then, we can see that the structure of the sportscasting industry—informed by the expectation of woman sportscaster emotion management—ensures that men are likely to continue to dominate the industry. When the industry conditions women in the industry to expect harassment and gendered mistreatment, it risks discouraging and losing talented women who are in or are considering careers as sportscasters.

Conclusion

Using the concepts of affect and emotion management, we are able to see how gendered neoliberalism is solidified as the glue that holds together the female sportscaster subjectivity in the contemporary moment. Without compliance with the neoliberal expectation that women sportscasters manage their emotions in a way that places the responsibility on them for managing others' behavior, the neoliberal female sportscaster cannot overcome double standards, bias, and harassment. Oddly, gendered neoliberalism not only relies on women sportscaster compliance within the context of sportscasting but is also bolstered by noncompliance. Those women who choose not to "check their dignity at the door" further prove that women need to adopt a neoliberal mindset if they are to thrive in the industry. No matter what choices women sportscasters make, the sophistication and insidiousness of a dependence on gendered neoliberalism serves to maintain the status quo. This sobering reality can therefore lead to only one conclusion: if women sportscasters are to achieve true equity within the industry, the industry itself must take responsibility for what happens to the women it puts on the air. This singular conclusion presents a series of far-reaching implications for the sportscasting industry and the way it trains, develops, hires, and retains on-air talent. I now turn to these implications in "The Postgame Show."

The Postgame Show

Although there can be little doubt that there are now more women in the sportscasting industry than there have ever been, the industry's reliance on gendered neoliberal discourse maintains the status quo with respect to true gender equity. Despite the increased visibility of women sportscasters, women in the industry are still expected to endure gendered and racialized double standards, bias, and harassment and to display an unaffected demeanor while doing so. The false positives brought to bear on the sportscasting industry and on women sportscasters as a result of gendered neoliberalism are analogous to a period of time in which the United States as a whole appeared to be on its way to making significant progress but actually held the status quo: the presidency of Barack Obama.

The forty-fourth president of the United States, Obama rode messages of hope and "Yes we can!" to the White House in 2008. After his inauguration, Obama successfully navigated the country out of a deep recession, presiding over the country for eight years. Obama, who was the United States' first Black, first non-white president, was diplomatic, well-spoken, handsome, and seemingly genuinely in love with his wife, Michelle, and daughters, Sasha and Malia. For those reasons alone Obama's absence has loomed large after his presidency expired and Donald Trump entered the White House, riding a completely different message.

Though Obama's election filled much of the country with hope that his administration would change American lives for the better, nearly four years after his presidency, the United States still found itself mired in many of the same obstacles it faced prior to his election. As of 2020, a great number of U.S. citizens still lacked sufficient medical coverage, insofar as a little more than 60 percent of individuals who file for bankruptcy do so under the weight of medical bills (Sainato 2019). An entire generation of Americans still have little spending power, having to fork over much of their income to pay off inordinate amounts of student loan debt. And, among other obstacles to national prosperity, U.S. law enforcement continues to disproportionately batter, incarcerate, and kill unarmed Black citizens. Regardless of how responsible one feels the U.S. government should be with respect to solving these issues, the fact that these issues remain despite eight years of the hope and visibility spurred on by the election of the country's first Black president is a sign that the United States has made little progress. In the years after Obama's presidency ended, the popular press debated the cause of the lack of change. Was it due to Obama's failure to push forward a Franklin Roosevelt–like transformative agenda (Manjoo 2019) or the fault of Congress, which, except for the first year or two of Obama's presidency, operated in such a way that it made it impossible for him even to appoint Supreme Court justices (Klein 2019)? Both arguments are convincing but are immaterial to this analogy. Ultimately, Obama's presidency shows us that it is not quite enough to espouse and champion messages of hope and empowerment or to elevate into highly visible positions those who come from marginalized social groups. Instead, in order to enact significant change, collective and corrective action must be taken by those in the majority as well as those in the minority. This is as true in sportscasting as it is in federal policy.

Through this Foucauldian project, I have attempted to show how the American female sportscaster subjectivity is constructed through gendered neoliberal discourses and how that subjectivity is brought to bear on the material experiences of women sportscasters in the United States. That is, women in the sportscasting industry are looked upon, thought of, spoken about, spoken to, and treated by men *and* women according to expectations that are narrow and contradictory. What most reinforces the status quo vis-à-vis gender in sportscasting, though, is the fact that gendered neoliberal discourses require women to take personal responsibility for navigating their own oppression. This absolves the industry of any responsibility for the way women sportscasters are treated and therefore leads to an industry that has little impetus to take steps toward making the industry more inclusive and supportive of women. As a result, the quantitative and discursive marginalization of women in the industry remains, and many women who are in the industry therefore suffer inequitable working conditions, forcing some women to choose to either voluntarily leave or not pursue careers in the industry. So sophisticated is gendered neoliberalism that its necessity is confirmed whenever women do choose to leave the industry. In making individual women sportscasters responsible for overcoming their own oppression, women sportscasters as a collective therefore never truly do overcome that oppression.

As the United States—and the world—watches sports every minute of every day, the representation of women in sportscasting affects the construction of gender (and race) in society at large. It is therefore urgent that the industry be more careful and intentional in how it represents women and gender on the air.

Industrial Implications

Unlike much of the extant scholarship that examines gender and sports media, *On the Sidelines* is not a quantitative study and is therefore neither a statistical analysis of survey entries nor a presentation of the results of a content analysis. In the absence of statistical data, I do not claim to prove, for example, that the majority of sports media consumers like hearing a woman's voice during a broadcast of a men's sporting event. In truth, given the extant scholarship, I would expect such a quantitative study, especially one that controls for social desirability bias, to demonstrate that sports media consumers, men and women, generally do *not* like hearing women. This would be my expectation because this attitude is apparent in the extant scholarship, in the discourse I analyzed, and in everyday conversations I have had, overheard, and read on online. The irregularity for women's voices during broadcasts of high-profile men's sports has been normalized and, as a result, sports media consumers have come to conclude that women either do not belong in the sportscasting booth or are out of place there.

For decades, sports media scholars have sought to affect change within the sports media industry by using quantitative data to prove the disparities that exist between, say, the coverage of men's and women's sports or the number of men and women working in the industry. The usage of quantitative research, while valuable, stems from a Western-centric notion that unbiased, objective truth can be obtained through positivism, embodied by quantitative research. I do not mean to suggest quantitative research is *never* effective, but as sports media scholars have come to realize, quantitative data have not affected much industrial change. This is perhaps due in part to the fact that such data mostly confirm what the industry already knows: the media do not provide equitable coverage of women's sports and men hold the majority of positions in the industry. To industry decision-makers, these statistics serve as evidence of "common-sense" realities that cannot be changed. It may also be that the statistics offered by sports media scholars do not offer a complete picture of the issue at hand. In the hypothetical study of media consumer willingness to listen to women's voices, if the results told us audiences were not willing, neither scholars nor the industry would know *why* this was the case. This would allow the industry to conveniently dismiss the bias for women's voices as a "scientifically proven" predisposition toward men's voices, a dismissal that avoids any acknowledgment of the industry's responsibility for the phenomenon.

To this end, I undertook this Foucauldian project to offer a more nuanced understanding of the issue of gender inequality in sportscasting. Foucault's power/knowledge paradigm does not claim to be able to prove a truth. In fact, it implicitly rejects the notions of proof because it also, more explicitly, rejects the notion of a singular truth. According to Foucault and his contemporaries, the truth is subjective insofar as the truths we hold are constructed by discourse and are therefore fluid. The experiences of the ten women I interviewed therefore cannot and should not be read as representative of the experiences of *all* women in the industry. However, this project was an attempt to demonstrate how the truths that many media consumers and industry professionals hold regarding women sportscasters have been iteratively constructed over time so as to appear real. In the case of the disdain for women's voices, using the power-knowledge paradigm, we now know this truth has likely been, at least in some small measure, learned through the exclusionary and narrow representation of women in the industry and is not a natural or monolithically imposed reality. More importantly, if these constructions of truth are fluid, then the upshot is that we can see a pathway through which many of the discursively constructed female sportscaster truths can be reverse engineered to construct *new* truths.

It would therefore behoove sports media organizations to be proactive. Bringing about change for the sake of greater equality for women would be a noble pursuit in and of itself. As Foucauldian power is fluid, though, there may come a time—however unlikely it seems at the moment—when structures of power and knowledge work against sportscasting's current gendered hierarchy. At such a point, those sports media organizations that have not made efforts toward greater equality for women may find that their practices regarding the treatment of women sportscasters (and even women's sports coverage) have become antiquated. As of 2020, there is evidence that the pendulum may already be swinging in that direction. Sports media critics have shined a light on a groundswell of support for ESPN's Doris Burke, at age fifty-two, to be promoted to the network's top NBA announcing crew as an analyst, with this support calling for Burke to replace former NBA player and coach Mark Jackson, whose analysis is deemed by many to be inferior to Burke's (Koo 2018). This potential development, both of the pendulum swing and of sports media organizations' failure to recognize it, could be much like the present moment in which sports media organizations are reeling as a result of not proactively adapting to the changes in media consumption brought about by digital technology.

Station and network executives may wonder if a discursive shift toward greater gender equality has not already taken place. Indeed, national sports networks like ESPN have made significant progress in integrating women into their studio shows like *SportsCenter* and in the booth. NBC Sports Network employed former U.S. Olympic women's hockey player AJ Mleczko as a booth analyst during its 2018 coverage of the NHL's Stanley Cup playoffs. FOX Sports utilized Aly Wagner, a former U.S. Women's National Team member, in a similar role during the 2018 FIFA Men's World Cup. Additionally, as evidenced by the women I interviewed, local television stations, sports talk radio stations, and regional sports networks have shown an increased willingness to hire women to cover sports.

However, this book's analysis of gendered neoliberalism demonstrates quantitative data can be deceiving. At its core, mediated sports remain a hostile space for women even though they have a larger presence in the industry than they have ever had. As sports journalist and women's sports advocate Jessica Luther told the *Chicago Tribune*:

> We, as a society, don't care very much about women. . . . Sometimes we do when it comes to viewing them as consumers, but in the sports world that seems to have little impact on changing the culture of sport to be more inclusive, safer, less misogynistic.
>
> The issues run deep here, and until these organizations and teams take them seriously we will always have this disconnect. Part of how to begin to fix that disconnect is to center (on) women when decisions are made. (Ryan 2016, para. 15–16)

Despite what gendered neoliberalism—through popular feminism—would have us believe, having more women on the air does not mean women in the industry automatically enjoy equitable working conditions. Station and network executives know this and their reliance on neoliberal logic as a means of addressing these issues makes them complicit. Consider this comment, as told by Jane, made by a male general manager to a group of new women hired by Jane's former full-time employer, a Western RSN:

> "I'm not saying I support this. I'm not saying I like it, but I'm saying this is how it is. . . . The reality is, we're going to put you all on TV, and your male counterparts are going to . . . be judged [by the audience] in a different way. The reality in this building, at our network, [is] you're probably also going to be held to that different standard, just because our product reflects our ratings and our approval ratings and viewership, so it's going to come down to being a business decision." He was making it very clear in my first week that, "Hey, I recognize this. It's not fair, but this is how it is, and you need to step up to that."

This general manager knows, at the very least, that women in the industry encounter double standards. Because of gendered neoliberalism, however, not only does he believe himself to be absolved of any responsibility for acting toward gender equity at his network but he is also permitted to use "ratings" and "business decision[s]" to justify making the women sportscasters at his station responsible for overcoming the gendered obstacles he readily acknowledges.

I am not so naïve as to not understand that ratings drive the sportscasting industry's decision-making. The industry's goal is to attract as many viewers and listeners to its content as possible to entice companies to advertise their products on their stations and networks. Through this process, electronic sports media organizations accrue advertising revenue, which pays for the organization's operating costs and fills the coffers of its stakeholders. Therefore, sportscasting is very much a capitalistic enterprise, which brings with it a litany of issues for those who are marginalized. Many may argue, justifiably, that the capitalistic nature of the industry precludes it from affecting change toward gender equality. In such an enterprise, all other objectives, including achieving gender equality, are typically secondary to making money or are in many cases nonexistent. Even if we acknowledge that the industry is capitalistic and therefore fraught with social baggage, we may still ask, what if accumulating good ratings and achieving gender equality need not be mutually exclusive? Further, what if pursuing gender equality could actually drive better ratings? If it is possible that media organizations can increase profits while also being socially conscious, to what extent does the industry need to be held accountable for the treatment of women sportscasters and women in society at large?

Audience research has long held that sports media consumers, an overstated percentage of whom are presumed to be heterosexual men, prefer their women sportscasters to look youthful, thin, and (usually) blonde and for their play-by-play announcers to be men. However, these learned *preferences* can be more accurately described as *expectations*. Just as long-standing practices have led sports media consumers to expect men, in the absence of women, to narrate sporting events, industry decision-makers can rewrite these expectations. As evidenced by the cases of Jessica Mendoza and Beth Mowins, many sports media consumers will reject efforts to this effect. Nevertheless, if sportscasting wants to be more inclusive of women, their voices, and their opinions, the industry must be willing to risk initially alienating much of its consumer base while also perhaps attracting new consumers. To be sure, the benefits of this approach will not likely be realized until some time after many of the current decision-makers have retired or moved on to other jobs. The task of reengineering audience expectations must begin, however, with decision-makers showing a steadfast willingness to eschew that status quo without being immediately and universally praised for doing so.

I also understand that, to some extent, efforts to affect greater equality for women in the industry have lagged because they have been politicized by partisan media outlets and politicians. In the current political climate, integrating women into the booth during men's sporting events is often viewed as being too "politically correct," or overly concerned with diversity and inclusion. Much of the backlash women like Mendoza and Mowins encounter stems from a politically driven and postfeminist notion that these women, and ESPN, have inexplicably and unnecessarily disavowed gender normative roles at the expense of otherwise qualified men. In other words, I understand the decision not to make changes toward greater equality for women in sportscasting is, by at least some small measure, driven by a desire to not alienate sports media consumers who may view any efforts toward diversity as unnecessarily virtuous and as running counter to their political ideals.

The strategy of hiring and appointing men to booth positions seems apolitical and safe for electronic media outlets, but in this political climate, taking a seemingly apolitical operational stance *is* political. The so-called neutral approach does nothing to subvert the status quo and is therefore unsurprisingly supported by politicians like Donald Trump. In response to ESPN personality Jemele Hill's claim that Trump is a "white supremacist," Trump (2017) referenced ESPN's declining ratings, stating: "ESPN is paying a really big price for its politics (and bad programming). People are dumping it in RECORD numbers" (emphasis in original). Although Trump referenced ESPN's programming, the fact he separated it with parentheses and the context in which he made the comment suggests a belief that the network's politics have primarily been detrimental to its ratings. While ESPN's ratings *have* been falling and the network *has* been losing subscribers, the extent to which its politics—which includes the network's propensity for discussing issues of gender and race in sport and its more inclusive hiring practices—have negatively impacted its ratings is unknown. Indeed, other factors such as media consumers' migration away from cable, toward streaming services such as Netflix and Hulu, have negatively impacted ratings and subscriptions for ESPN and other relatively apolitical cable networks such as TBS, TNT, and Discovery ("Competitive Info" 2017). Nevertheless, many observers accepted as truth that ESPN's perceived liberal bias is the primary factor in its ratings decline (Clavio and Vooris 2017). Additionally, many political pundits, including Rush Limbaugh, have pointed to ESPN's inclusive hiring practices as evidence of a network that is liberal and overly virtuous (DailyRushBo 2017).

Just as political truths can be discursively constructed and learned through messages and practices, media consumer expectations of who is qualified to provide commentary and narrations for certain sports can also be constructed and learned. To that end, I present a series of suggestions for the sportscasting industry that might make it a more inclusive space for more women and normalize the presence of women in the industry. I offer these suggestions with the caveats that their desired results will take time to be realized, that they may not agree with the attitudes embedded in society at large, and, as a result, that they may initially alienate some media consumers. However, if media consumers are alienated by the presence of a woman on a baseball broadcast simply because she is a woman, I argue that is precisely why these changes are worth considering. Mediated sports are often marketed by sports organizations and media outlets as a force that can unify people of varying identities for the benefit of society at large. Is that marketing, however, disingenuous if the industry does not utilize and support its employees according to these same ideals? If it potentially alienates a large portion of its consumer base (women)? If it is disingenuous, does that render moot sports' potential for affecting social change?

To wit, during the 2018 FIFA Men's World Cup, a supposedly unifying mega-event, a Colombian reporter, Julieth González Therán, was sexually assaulted on live television (Gardner 2018), and in Britain it was considered controversial for the BBC to employ women as analysts during its coverage of the tournament (Blum 2018). The backlash against the BBC analysts may have been inevitable and comes from an effort to integrate more women into the coverage of a men's sporting event. Also, sexual assaults such as that encountered by González Therán happen to women across many institutions, not just sportscasting. Nevertheless, these events drew attention away from what is supposed to be a celebration of competition and multiculturalism and instead shed light once again on the issues women in sportscasting often encounter. Even beyond the United States, the industry bears at least some responsibility for both incidents, given sportscasting's historically problematic representation of women. Is the industry comfortable with that culpability?

Improving Conditions for Women Sportscasters

The goal of the suggestions I make here is to acclimate the audience to listening to women narrate and analyze men's sports while also making sportscasting a more enjoyable and attractive industry for women to work in.

Addressing the Double Standard of Appearance

Because the double standard of appearance is the foundation upon which so many of the other obstacles are built, industry decision-makers need to be intentional about deprioritizing appearance in the hiring and retention of female (and male) sportscasters. This does not mean that universally attractive women sportscasters—those who are young, thin, long-haired, and white—should be disqualified from future job openings. Instead, this simply means that women sportscasters who are not universally attractive should not be disqualified or viewed as less qualified than someone who is deemed to be more attractive yet has inferior skills, knowledge, and experience. In addition, as the current expectations of woman sportscaster appearance are based on Anglocentric ideals of feminine beauty, non-white women sportscasters should not be discouraged from, among other things, wearing their hair however they are accustomed to doing so. As the case of Sonya Forte Duhé showed us in chapter 1, the notion that women of all ethnicities should straighten their hair needs to be unlearned at all levels and in all realms, including and especially journalism education. Not only is it racist to suggest to non-white women that natural hair is unkempt or that straight hair is more presentable, it also takes away these women's agency and identity. Few people would want to go on air with unkempt hair, and women of all races closely identify with their hairstyles. To consider non-white and non-straight hairstyles unkempt and to universally suggest they be straightened, then, is to also whitewash a woman's identity. While some non-white women may prefer to wear their hair straight, giving women in general the ability to choose their hairstyles will normalize natural non-Anglo hair. This normalization may be an unpleasant shock to consumers accustomed to seeing women sportscasters with straightened hair, but that is partly why the change is necessary. Then again, given preliminary discussions I have had with Black women newscasters, viewers may not be as offended by non-Anglo hairstyles as industry decision-makers would have women believe.

Deprioritizing attractiveness and an adherence to idealized white femininity among woman sportscasters would have many other positive effects, aside from normalizing non-Anglo hairstyles. Perhaps the most important effect of such a maneuver would be that it would, in theory, open the door for women who, because of their identities, do not meet the normalized standards of attractiveness. Specifically, I mean non-white, non-cisgender, non-heterosexual, and non-thin women along with people who are nonbinary or genderqueer. This is not to suggest that people who fall into these categories are not attractive in their own right. Instead, I mean to suggest that a deprioritization of appearance will necessarily negate normative white, cisgender, heterosexual, and feminine notions of what constitutes attractiveness. These notions have typically excluded the women I just described.

Perhaps the most wide-reaching effect of deprioritizing appearance would be the increased perceived credibility of women sportscasters. This is not to suggest attractive women cannot be credible. Instead, I argue, as I did in chapter 1, that the industry's prioritization of appearance gives the appearance of a lack of skill among those women who are hired. Although the relative invisibility of women in sports in general does women no favors, the sports media complex can help construct woman sportscasters as knowledgeable, trustworthy sources of sports information by hiring those with the most knowledge and the best abilities. This would help to eliminate, among other things, the assumed promiscuity and gendered skepticism I described in chapter 1.

Decision-makers will attempt to justify the appearance double standard by citing the will of their audiences. While it is true that many sports media consumers might be initially surprised and perhaps even turned off by a deprioritization of Anglocentric appearance for women sportscasters, decision-makers need to be undeterred in the face of any such criticism. Media organizations have sometimes shown a willingness to remain steadfastly committed to gender equity, as evidenced by their refusal to relent despite the criticism they have faced while incorporating women like Mendoza and Mowins into the broadcast booth. To justify a turn toward deprioritizing appearance as a way of fostering more equitable hiring and retention among woman sportscasters, decision-makers would do well to heed the comments made by veteran sportscaster Jim Lampley. As cited in chapter 2, Lampley thought it dubious that the presence of traditionally attractive women motivated men to watch sports on television. Sports media consumers primarily watch sports programming because of their interest in sports, not because of the people who appear on camera. There are other media industries that rely on the presentation of attractive women to draw an audience. Sports media organizations are not among those industries and need not try to be.

Responding to Harassment

Although the appearance and credibility double standards inform the harassment women in the sportscasting industry endure, harassment is very much part of a larger societal issue that needs addressing in and out of sports media. Still, sportscasting can aid in ending the normalization of gendered workplace and online harassment. First, women should not feel ashamed or at risk of losing their jobs because they menstruate, have suffered a miscarriage, or have become pregnant. Given the illegality of such discrimination, this suggestion would seem to go without saying, but the discourse analyzed in chapter 3 implies that is not the case.

To help curb this type of workplace harassment, then, I suggest that media organizations, especially larger ones with more resources and more women employees (such as national networks and RSNs) establish a role that is independent of the human resources department but performs a similar function as a university's Title IX office.

In sportscasting, the person in this role would be tasked with ensuring that the media organization complies with all EEOC regulations vis-à-vis harassment (based on gender and other protected classes). To eliminate potential conflicts of interest, the person in this role would act independently—insofar as they would not report to anyone, save for the organization's highest-ranking official. This position may seem unnecessary, given the universal presence of a human resources office. However, given the predominance of men in sportscasting, it stands to reason that such a position, one that can act with relative independence and therefore has no social capital to give or take away from women sportscasters employed by the organization, might be necessary.

Aside from administrative changes, the industry can help curb the harassment of women sportscasters by fully supporting women when they say they have been harassed. This means not dismissing their feelings or normalizing their harassers' behaviors. Women who are harassed by the athletes and coaches they cover should be allowed to distance themselves and should not be forced by the industry to succumb to pressure from superiors or sources to do otherwise. Further, sources and superiors who do harass woman sportscasters should be dealt with. To ignore their behavior normalizes it and leaves open the possibility they may harass other women. In the case of sources, a lack of acknowledgment makes it impossible for women to cover them or their teams. Finally, a commitment to ending harassment against women sportscasters means that male superiors and peers need to also speak out against—rather than ignore or, in Clay Travis and Jason Whitlock's case, trivialize—observed acts of workplace and online harassment and to educate their audiences as to why harassment is wrong. To not speak out is tantamount to complicity, and to suggest that men and women suffer the same type of harassment or that one is worse than the other is also complicit. Addressing these practices, meanwhile, will help lessen the emotional load on women in the industry, which, in turn, will make it more desirable for women who are considering entering or staying in the business. This increased desirability would theoretically help increase the visibility of women in the industry and potentially attract consumers who are looking for balanced commentary, in a representational sense. Since we know online harassment to be a manifestation of popular misogyny, sports media organizations, especially those with abundant resources, need to make a bigger political and financial investment in curbing this phenomenon.

Making Women More Visible

Another action that sportscasting could take to make women in the industry more visible *and* normalize their presence would be to include more women's voices not just in live sports broadcasts but also in presentations of historicized sporting events. These presentations should include sports documentaries, which, thanks to the proliferation of regularly televised docuseries such as ESPN's *30 for 30*, NFL Network's *A Football Life*, and HBO's *24/7* have become an essential part of sports media consumption. Taking up this practice would serve multiple purposes. First, it would help prime the sports media consumer base for hearing women's voices during broadcasts and other sports media products. Having women narrate historicized sports might also encourage more women to enter the field in roles in which they primarily use their voices (play-by-play or color commentary). This strategy may also encourage more industry executives and college programs to afford women the opportunity to train for the broadcast booth. In essence, the premise behind this strategy of making women's voices more prominent would be to make it more feasible for consumers and sports media personnel to imagine hearing (and enjoying) women provide commentary during sporting events.

These three non-exhaustive areas of emphasis all serve the same purpose: to take an intentional approach to "shaking up" the status quo and to reengineer media consumers' expectations. Indeed, such a multipronged approach would more effectively combat gendered neoliberalism, which maintains, and is to some extent maintained by, sports media's status quo. As I wrote earlier in this volume, the mutually informing relationship between sports media and gendered neoliberalism renders sports media a highly visible *gendered* and *gendering* space. As such, the industry is responsible not only for the treatment of the women it employs but also for the construction of gender in Western society. If women sportscasters are expected to navigate apparent double standards, overcome deeply rooted biases for certain positions, and endure disproportionate gendered harassment and affective labor with few to no structural interventions, then for a large number of the millions of folks who regularly consume sports media, those expectations continue to be commonsensical for women in their everyday lives.

Sports media organizations should therefore act accordingly.

Notes

Preface

1. Jemele Hill and ESPN agreed to part ways in 2018, shortly after Jimmy Pitaro took over at ESPN.

The Pregame Show

1. Dan McNeil publicly apologized to Maria Taylor before ultimately losing his job.

2. At the time it was published, Jason Whitlock's piece on Maria Taylor was available for all to read. Upon searching for the article on November 30, 2020, I found that the article was placed behind a paywall. I wrote about that piece and offered direct quotes on September 27 of that year, before the paywall went up. For reasons that should be obvious, I have avoided subscribing to Outkick.com and can therefore no longer verify which paragraph contained this quote.

3. Whitlock wrote another piece the next day on ESPN personality Katie Nolan titled "Katie Nolan Represents the Elimination of America's Meritocracy and Exposes the Fraudulence of Her Supporters."

4. *Cisgender*: a term used when someone self-identifies as the gender that mirrors the sex they were assigned at birth.

5. The broadcast media (and therefore "broadcasting") only include over-the-air television (ABC, NBC, CBS) and terrestrial (i.e., not satellite or streaming) radio.

6. Parasocial interactions are one-sided interactions media consumers have with the people they see on television or in films, much in the same way some viewers closely followed *The Oprah Winfrey Show* because they formed a one-sided bond with the show's host.

7. Title IX of the Education Amendments Act of 1972 states: "No person in the United States shall, on the basis of sex, be excluded from participation in, be denied the benefits of, or be subjected to discrimination under any education program or activity receiving Federal financial assistance." Participation in interscholastic athletics falls under the purview of this law.

8. After 2008 Papper stopped including sports television personnel in his annual diversity survey. In personal communication with me, Papper stated that he did not receive enough participation among sportscasters to make them worth including in future surveys. I found no other statistics regarding diversity in sports broadcast news.

9. Patricia's mother is white and her father is Black.

10. As of November 2020, the PSA had accumulated more than 4.6 million views on YouTube.

2. Sportscasting's Glass Booth

1. Bell, who was never a professional athlete, was suspended for three days for his comments regarding Mendoza.

3. Gendered Harassment in Sportscasting

1. A sports director at a local television station usually oversees the station's sports department, particularly its on-air personnel, and in many cases is the station's lead sports anchor.

References

Abelson, Jenn. 2017. "At ESPN, the Problems for Women Run Deep." *Boston Globe.* https://www.bostonglobe.com/sports/2017/12/14/women-who-worked-espn -say-its-problems-far-beyond-barstool-sports/L1v9HJIvtnHuBPiMru6yGM /story.html.

Ahmed, Sara. 2014. *The Cultural Politics of Emotion.* 2nd ed. Edinburgh: Edinburgh University Press.

Alindogan, Marah. 2016. "Erin Andrews Makes Surprising Admission about 'DWTS' Finale Dress." AOL. https://www.aol.com/article/2016/05/25/erin-andrews-makes -surprising-admission-about-dwts-finale-dres/21383904/#.

Antunovic, Dunja. 2015. "'Just Another Story': Sports Journalists' Memories of Title IX and Women's Sport." *Communication and Sport.* DOI: 10.1177/2167479515603956.

Banet-Weiser, Sarah. 2017. "Commentary: When 'Nice Guys' Turn Out to Be Sexual Predators." *Fortune.* https://fortune.com/2017/11/30/matt-lauer-sexual -harassment-nice-guys/.

———. 2018. *Empowered: Popular Feminism and Popular Misogyny.* Durham: Duke University Press.

Banet-Weiser, Sarah, Rosalind Gill, and Catherine Rottenberg. 2019. "Postfeminism, Popular Feminism, and Neoliberal Feminism? Sarah Banet-Weiser, Rosalind Gill and Catherine Rottenberg in Conversation." *Feminist Theory.* DOI: 10.1177/1464700119842555.

Barstool Sports (@barstoolsports). 2014. "Linda Cohn has been MILFing EXTRA hard on Sportscenter lately." Tweet. https://twitter.com/barstoolsports/status /541406440288960512.

Bien-Aime, Steve. 2016. "AP Stylebook Normalizes Sports as a Male Space." *Newspaper Research Journal* 37, no. 1: 1–14.

Blum, Ronald. 2018. "Women Make World Cup Television History in the US, UK, Germany." *Chicago Tribune.* http://www.chicagotribune.com/90minutes/ct -90mins-women-make-world-cup-television-history-in-the-us-uk-germany -20180630-story.html.

Boutilier, Mary, and Lucinda SanGiovanni. 1983. *The Sporting Woman.* Champaign IL: Human Kinetics.

Butler, Jess. 2013. "For White Girls Only? Postfeminism and the Politics of Inclusion." *Feminist Formations* 25, no. 1: 35–58.

Cahn, Susan K. 1994. *Coming on Strong: Gender and Sexuality in Twentieth-Century Women's Sports*. New York: Free Press.

Carrington, Ben. 2010. *Race, Sport and Politics: The Sporting Black Diaspora*. London: Sage.

Chemaly, Soraya. 2014. "There Is No Comparing Male and Female Harassment Online." *Time*. http://time.com/3305466/male-female-harassment-online/.

Clavio, Galen, and Ryan Vooris. 2017. "ESPN and the Hostile Media Effect." *Communication and Sport*. DOI: 10.1177/2167479517739835.

CNN. 2019. "'To silence women when it comes to sports . . . is also silencing women from commenting on what's happening in this country.' Sports journalist @ JulieDiCaro, on Trump's pick for the Fed—Stephen Moore—having made sexist comments in several past columns." Tweet and video. https://twitter.com /CNN/status/1121147961151512578.

Cohn, Linda. 2008. "Sex and the Female Sportscaster." In *Cohn-head: A No-Holds-Barred Account of Breaking into the Boys' Club*. Kindle version. Guilford CT: Lyons Press.

Cohn, Linda (@lindacohn). 2014. "At least @DavidLloydESPN was hard at work during commercial break of @SportsCenter. I was compelled to strike a pose." Tweet. https://twitter.com/lindacohn/status/540645030072168448.

———. 2016. "This one is the top seller so far. Do you agree? Official autographs on sale @lcoautographs http://ow.ly/ZWgVF." Tweet. https://twitter.com/lindacohn /status/713518431081877504.

Collins, Patricia H. 2014. *Black Sexual Politics: African-Americans, Gender, and the New Racism*. New York: Routledge.

"Competitive Info: TV Posts Double-Digit Ratings Declines." 2017. *Inside Radio*. http://www.insideradio.com/free/competitive-info-tv-posts-double-digit-ratings -declines/article_8f9de456-e488-11e7-9c9f-e3a391cca3de.html.

Cooky, Cheryl, Michael Messner, and Robin Hextrum. 2013. "Women Play Sport, but Not on TV: A Longitudinal Study of Televised News Media." *Communication and Sport* 1, no. 3: 203–30.

Cooky, Cheryl, Michael Messner, and Michela Musto. 2015. "'It's Dude Time!': A Quarter Century of Excluding Women's Sports in Televised News and Highlight Shows." *Communication and Sport* 3, no. 3: 261–87.

Copeland, Libby. 2013. "Female TV Newscasters and the Sleeveless Sheath Dress." *Slate*. http://www.slate.com/articles/double_x/doublex/2013/04/female_tv_newscasters _and_the_sleeveless_sheath_dress.html.

Crags, Tommy. 2009. "The First Sideline Reporter: 'All of This Was Just Nonsense.'" *Deadspin*. https://deadspin.com/5323838/the-first-sideline-reporter-all-of-this -was-just-nonsense.

Cramer, Judith. 1994. "Conversations with Women Sports Journalists." In *Women, Media and Sport: Challenging Gender Values*, edited by P. Creedon, 159–80. Thousand Oaks CA: Sage.

Creedon, Pamela J. 1994. "From Whalebone to Spandex: Women and Sports Journalism in American Magazine, Photography and Broadcasting." In *Women, Media, and Sport: Challenging Gender Values*, edited by P. Creedon, 108–58. Thousand Oaks CA: Sage.

——. 1998. "Women, Sport, and Media Institutions: Issues in Sports Journalism and Marketing." In *MediaSport*, edited by L. A. Wenner, 88–99. London: Routledge.

Creedon, Pamela J., and Roseanna M. Smith. 2007. "Women Journalists in Toyland and the Locker Room: It's All about the Money." In *Women in Mass Communication*, edited by P. J. Creedon and J. Cramer, 147–58. Thousand Oaks CA: Sage.

Cummins, R. Glenn, Monica Ortiz, and Andrea Rankine. 2018. "'Elevator Eyes' in Sports Broadcasting: Visual Objectification of Male and Female Sports Reporters." *Communication and Sport* 7, no. 6: 789–810.

DailyRushBo. 2017. "Limbaugh: 'Poor' Sergio Dipp Had No Business Being Put on the Sideline." https://www.youtube.com/watch?v=Rbp5GKcNjr8.

Davis, Daniel C., and Janielle Krawczyk. 2010. "Female Sportscaster Credibility: Has Appearance Taken Precedence?" *Journal of Sports Media* 5, no. 2: 1–34.

Deitsch, Richard. 2014. "Erin Andrews Replaces Pam Oliver on Fox's No. 1 NFL team." *Sports Illustrated*. http://www.si.com/nfl/2014/07/14/pam-oliver-erin-andrews-fox.

——. 2017. "Revisiting Sexual Harassment of Female Sports Reporters and Media Members." *Sports Illustrated*. https://www.si.com/tech-media/2017/11/26/female-sports-reporters-sexual-harassment-media-circus.

Deliovsky, Katerina. 2010. *White Femininity: Race, Gender, and Power*. Halifax, Nova Scotia: Fernwood.

DiCaro, Julie. 2015. "Threats, Vitriol, Hate: Ugly Truth about Women in Sports and Social Media." *Sports Illustrated*. http://www.si.com/cauldron/2015/09/27/twitter-threats-vile-remarks-women-sports-journalists.

——. 2017. "Safest Bet in Sports: Men Complaining about a Female Announcer's Voice." *New York Times*. https://www.nytimes.com/2017/09/18/sports/nfl-beth-mowins-julie-dicaro.html.

——. 2020. "Since Half of NFL Fans Are Women, How 'bout Putting One in the Booth for 'Monday Night Football'?" *Deadspin*. https://deadspin.com/since-half-of-nfl-fans-are-women-how-bout-putting-one-1843548549.

Duffy, Ty. 2014. "Artie Lange's Slave Sex Fantasy Tweets about ESPN's Cari Champion Offended Just about Everyone." *The Big Lead*. http://thebiglead.com/2014/11/05/artie-lange-slave-sex-tweets-about-espn-cari-champion-offended-just-about-everyone/.

Duncan, Margaret C., Kerry Jensen, and Michael A. Messner. 1993. "Separating the Men from the Girls: The Gendered Language of Televised Sports." *Gender and Society* 7: 121–37.

D'Zurilla, Christie. 2014. "Artie Lange Explains His Racist Sex Fantasy about ESPN's Cari Champion." *Los Angeles Times*. http://www.latimes.com/entertainment

/gossip/la-et-mg-artie-lange-cari-champion-racist-sex-fantasy-twitter-espn
-20141105-story.html.

Eastman, Susan T., and Andrew C. Billings. 2000. "Sportscasting and Sports Reporting: The Power of Gender Bias." *Journal of Sport and Social Issues* 24, no. 2: 192–213.

EEOC. 2018. "Harassment Policy." Equal Employment Opportunity Commission. https://www.eeoc.gov/laws/types/harassment.cfm.

Ekman, Paul. 1992. "An Argument for Basic Emotions." *Cognition and Emotion* 6, no. 3/4: 169–200.

ESPN. 2019. "Katie Nolan Joins Secret Society of Women in Sports Media | Always Late with Katie Nolan." https://www.youtube.com/watch?v=BuNRvHt8tlY.

———. 2020. "TV Pioneer Phyllis George, Co-host of 'The NFL Today,' Dies at 70." ESPN.com. https://www.espn.com/nfl/story/_/id/29184112/tv-pioneer-phyllis -george-co-host-nfl-today-dies-70.

Etling, Laurence W., and Raymond Young. 2007. "Sexism and the Authoritativeness of Female Sportscasters." *Communication Research Reports* 24, no. 2: 121–30.

Etling, Laurence W., Raymond W. Young, William V. Faux, and Joseph C. Mitchell. 2011. "Just Like One of the Guys? Perceptions of Male and Female Sportscaster Voices." *Journal of Sports Media* 6, no. 2: 1–21.

Everbach, Tracy. 2018. "'I Realized It Was about Them . . . Not Me': Women Sports Journalists and Harassment." In *Mediating Misogyny: Gender, Technology, and Harassment*, edited by J. R. Vickery and T. Everbach, 131–49. London: Palgrave Macmillan.

Everett, Cristina. 2010. "Erin Andrews: 'I Didn't Speak' with Elisabeth Hasselbeck When She Tried Calling Me to Apologize." *New York Daily News*. http://www .nydailynews.com/entertainment/gossip/erin-andrews-didn-speak-elisabeth -hasselbeck-calling-apologize-article-1.180253.

Feder, Robert. 2015. "Comcast SportsNet Extracts Apology for The Score's Sexist Tweets." http://www.robertfeder.com/2015/03/26/comcast-sportsnet-extracts -apology-for-scores-sexist-tweets/.

Feitelberg, John. 2014. "minihane." https://www.youtube.com/watch?v=62o3j1ukOLo.

"Female Sports Writers Denied Entry to Locker Room at Lucas Oil Stadium." 2015. *Sports Illustrated*. https://www.si.com/nfl/2015/10/04/female-sportswriters-held -out-indianapolis-colts-locker-room.

Finn, Chad. 2014. "Fox Pulls All Advertising on WEEI, Entercom." *Boston Globe*. https://www.bostonglobe.com/sports/2014/07/25/fox-pulls-all-advertising-weei -parent-company-entercom/WpPEiZSjqvqHAfjk9XuLpK/story.html.

Fornoff, Susan. 1993. *Lady in the Locker Room*. Champaign IL: Sagamore.

Foucault, Michel. 1978. *The History of Sexuality: Vol. 1, An Introduction*. New York: Vintage.

———. 1980. *Power/Knowledge: Selected Interviews and Other Writings: 1972–1977*. Edited by C. Gordon. New York: Pantheon.

FOX Sports. 2015. "Clay Travis Has His Mom Read Mean Tweets." https://www .youtube.com/watch?v=-EkOK3WH9Lo.

Garber, Greg. 2002. "Landmark Law Faces New Challenges Even Now." http://espn .go.com/gen/womenandsports/020619title9.html.

Gardner, Steve. 2018. "Female Reporter at World Cup Sexually Assaulted during a Live Broadcast." *USA Today*. https://www.usatoday.com/story/sports/soccer/2018 /06/20/female-reporter-sexually-assaulted-world-cup-broadcast/719208002/.

Genz, Stephanie, and Benjamin A. Brabon. 2018. *Postfeminism: Cultural Texts and Theories*. 2nd ed. Edinburgh: Edinburgh University Press.

Gerbner, George. 1978. "The Dynamics Of Cultural Resistance." In *Women in the Mass Media*, edited by G. Tuchman, 46–50. New York: Oxford University Press.

Gill, Rosalind. 2007. *Gender and the Media*. Cambridge: Polity Press.

Gill, Rosalind, and Christina Scharff. 2011. "Introduction." In *New Femininities: Postfeminism, Neoliberalism and Subjectivity*, edited by R. Gill and C. Scharff, 1–7. New York: Palgrave Macmillan.

Gordon, Alison. 1984. *Foul Balls: Five Years in the American League*. Toronto: McClelland and Stewart.

Gottlieb, Doug (@GottliebShow). 2020. "Why does Maria Taylor have a vote? Real question. She is a studio host/sideline reporter in her first year covering the NBA. She works a ton, not just on the league. No reason for her to have a vote." Tweet. https://twitter.com/GottliebShow/status/1307386119810498560.

Guerrero, Lisa (@4lisaguerrero). 2017. "Lots of people thru the years have asked me why I left sports broadcasting. In this wonderful article about #MeToo in Sports by @Lisa_Olson1 I finally share one of the many reasons why." Tweet. https:// twitter.com/4lisaguerrero/status/944282276984057856.

———. 2020a. "An absolute trailblazer who carved a path for women in sports. My condolences to Phyllis George's loved ones tonight. May she Rest In Peace." Tweet. https://twitter.com/4lisaguerrero/status/1261850635772649472.

———. 2020b. "Was sent this from 2010. Interesting to see the pic they used of me after over a decade on the field covering sports. This is one of the reasons I'm glad I moved on to investigative journalism." Tweet. https://twitter.com /4lisaguerrero/status/1262069790996180994.

Hale, Charles. 2006. "Activist Research v. Cultural Critique: Indigenous Land Rights and the Contradictions of Politically Engaged Anthropology." *Cultural Anthropology* 21, no. 1: 96–120.

Hardin, Marie, Julie Dodd, and Kimberly Lauffer. 2006. "Passing It On: The Reinforcement of Male Hegemony in Sports Journalism Textbooks." *Mass Communication and Society* 9, no. 4: 429–46.

Hardin, Marie, and Stacie Shain. 2006. "Feeling Much Smaller Than You Know You Are: The Fragmented Professional Identity of Female Sports Journalists." *Critical Studies in Media Communication* 23, no. 4: 322–38.

Hardin, Marie, and Erin Whiteside. 2006. "Fewer Women, Minorities Work in Sports Departments." *Newspaper Research Journal* 27, no. 2: 38–51.

Harrison, Guy. 2018. "'You Have to Have Thick Skin': Embracing the Affective Turn as an Approach to Investigating the Treatment of Women Working in Sports Media." *Feminist Media Studies*. DOI: 10.1080/14680777.2018.1498123.

———. 2019. "'We Want to See You Sex It Up and Be Slutty': Post-Feminism and Sports Media's Appearance Double Standard." *Critical Studies in Media Communication* 36, no. 2: 140–55.

———. 2020. "The Past Week in the Life of Maria Taylor Embodied Life as a Woman in Sports Media." *On the Sidelines* (blog). https://onthesidelinesbook.wordpress .com/2020/09/27/the-past-week-in-the-life-of-maria-taylor-embodies-life-as -a-woman-in-sports-media/.

Harrison, Guy, Ann Pegoraro, Miles Romney, and Kevin Hull. 2019. "The 'Angry Black Woman': How Race, Gender, and American Politics Influenced User Discourse Surrounding the Jemele Hill Controversy." *Howard Journal of Communication* 31, no. 2: 137–49.

Hill, Tim. 2015. "Jessica Mendoza Receives Sexist Backlash after Calling MLB Playoff Game." *Guardian*. https://www.theguardian.com/sport/2015/oct/07/jessica -mendoza-espn-mlb-yankees-astros.

Hochschild, Arlie R. 1979. "Emotion Working, Feeling Rules, and Social Structure." *American Journal of Sociology* 85, no. 3: 551–75.

———. 1983. *The Managed Heart: Commercialization of Human Feeling*. Berkeley: University of California Press.

Hollywood Reporter. 2015. "Michelle Beadle on Women Sportscasters: We're More Than Just Sideline Reporters." https://www.youtube.com/watch?v=inrBuvtIzeg.

hooks, bell. 1990. *Yearning: Race, Gender, and Cultural Politics*. Boston: South End.

Hull, Kevin, Miles Romney, Ann Pegoraro, and Guy Harrison. 2019. "'It's Funny to Hear a Female Talk about Routes': Social Media Reaction to Cam Newton's Comments about a Woman Reporter." *Journal of Social Media in Society* 8, no. 1: 35–54.

"The Internet Claims This White Sports Reporter's Waist-Length Box Braids Proves 'White Privilege.'" 2018. BET. https://www.bet.com/news/national/2018/08/25 /fox-news-reporter-braids.html.

Jones, Bomani (@bomani_jones). 2017. "i'm the skinniest dude in the world with a messed up grill—under construction—and hairline AND THEY PUT ME ON TV. think about that." Tweet. https://twitter.com/bomani_jones/status /848895266681966592.

Just Not Sports. 2016. "#MoreThanMean—Women in Sports 'Face' Harassment." https://www.youtube.com/watch?v=9tU-D-m2JY8.

Kaminski, Kaitlyn. 2014. "Women in Sports Media Gain Ground, but It's an Uphill Climb." *Seattle Times*. http://blogs.seattletimes.com/take2/2014/09/11/women -in-sports-media-gain-ground-but-its-an-uphill-climb/.

Kane, Mary Jo, and Lisa J. Disch. 1993. "Sexual Violence and the Reproduction of Male Power in the Locker Room: The 'Lisa Olson Incident.'" *Sociology of Sport Journal* 10: 331–52.

Kennedy, Helen. 2010. "ESPN Suspends Tony Kornheiser for Comments about Sportscenter Anchor Hannah Storm's Wardrobe." *New York Daily News*. http://www.nydailynews.com/sports/espn-suspends-tony-kornheiser-comments-sportscenter-anchor-hannah-storm-wardrobe-article-1.195854.

Kerr-Dineen, Luke. 2017. "Barstool Chief to Sam Ponder: 'Sex It Up and Be Slutty.'" *USA Today*. https://www.usatoday.com/story/sports/ftw/2017/10/17/barstool-chief-to-sam-ponder-in-2014-stop-showing-pictures-of-your-ugly-kid-sex-it-up-and-be-slutty/106729640/.

King, Martin L. 1963. *Letter from a Birmingham Jail*. https://www.africa.upenn.edu/Articles_Gen/Letter_Birmingham.html.

Klein, Ezra. 2019. "Leftists, Liberals, and Neoliberals Share the Same Problem: Congress." *Vox*. https://www.vox.com/policy-and-politics/2019/9/20/20874204/obama-farhad-manjoo-neoliberalism-financial-crisissanders-warren.

Knight, Molly (@molly_knight). 2015. "This guy is so INCENSED that a woman would be allowed near sports that he has tweeted at 59(!) strangers about it." Tweet. https://twitter.com/molly_knight/status/651587148768919554.

Koo, Ben. 2018. "Doris Burke Is an Obvious Upgrade Over Mark Jackson, But . . ." *Awful Announcing*. https://awfulannouncing.com/espn/doris-burke-is-an-obvious-upgrade-to-mark-jackson-but.html.

Lapchick, Richard, Austin Bloom, Saahil Marfatia, Bharath Balasundaram, Abdul Bello-Malabu, Tais Cotta, Evin Morrison, Mark Mueller, Mary Mulcahy, Stanley Sylverain, Todd Currie, and Tynelle-Taylor Chase. 2018. *The 2018 Associated Press Sports Editors Racial and Gender Report Card*. https://43530132-36e9-4f52-811a-182c7a91933b.filesusr.com/ugd/7d86e5_9dca4bc2067241cdba67aa2f1b09fd1b.pdf.

Laucella, Pamela. 2014. "The Evolution from Print to Online Platforms for Sports Journalism." In *Routledge Handbook of Sports and New Media*, edited by A. C. Billings and M. Hardin. New York: Routledge.

Lee, Ashley. 2019. "Oscar Nominations Shut Out Female Directors—Again." *Los Angeles Times*. https://www.latimes.com/entertainment/la-et-mn-oscars-nominations-female-directors-20190122-story.html.

Loede, Matt. 2020. "Chicago Radio Talker Fired after 'Degrading and Humiliating' Tweet about ESPN's Maria Taylor." *Sports Illustrated*. https://www.si.com/mlb/indians/news/chicago-radio-talker-fired-after-degrading-and-humiliating-tweet-about-espns-maria-taylor.

Manjoo, Farhad. 2019. "Barack Obama's Biggest Mistake." *New York Times*. https://www.nytimes.com/2019/09/18/opinion/obama-2008-financial-crisis.html.

Martin, Jill. 2017. "Reporter: NFL Network Asked If She Plans on 'Getting Knocked Up.'" CNN. http://www.cnn.com/2017/12/13/sport/lindsay-mccormick-nfl-network-interview/index.html.

McCombs, Maxwell E., and Donald L. Shaw. 1972. "The Agenda-Setting Function of Mass Media." *Public Opinion Quarterly* 36, no. 2: 176–87.

McRobbie, Angela. 2004. "Post-feminism and Popular Culture." *Feminist Media Studies* 4, no. 3: 255–64.

———. 2011. "Preface." In *Femininities: Postfeminism, Neoliberalism and Subjectivity*, edited by R. Gill and C. Scharff, xi–xv. New York: Palgrave Macmillan.

Mead, Doug. 2010. "Twelve Women Who Pioneered the Era of Female Sports Broadcasters." *Bleacher Report*. https://bleacherreport.com/articles/440556-twelve-women-who-pioneered-the-era-of-female-sports-broadcasters.

Messner, Michael A., Margaret C. Duncan, and Cheryl Cooky. 2003. "Silence, Sports Bras, and Wrestling Porn: Women in Televised Sports News And Highlights Shows." *Journal of Sport and Social Issues* 27, no. 1: 38–51.

Miloch, Kimberly, Paul Pedersen, Michael Smucker, and Warren Whisenant. 2005. "The Current State of Women Print Journalists: An Analysis of the Status and Careers of Females in Newspaper Sports Departments." *Public Organization Review* 5: 219–32.

Moon, Dreama. 1999. "White Enculturation and Bourgeois Ideology: The Discursive Production of 'Good (White) Girls.'" In *Whiteness: The Social Communication of Social Identity*, edited by T. Nakayama and J. Martin. Thousand Oaks CA: Sage.

Mowins, Beth (@bethmowins). 2020. "Watching this crew every Sunday got a little girl like me to dreaming. Can I be a sportscaster like her? Thank you Phyllis George @CBSSports." Tweet. https://twitter.com/bethmowins/status/1261808715163811840.

Musto, Michela, Cheryl Cooky, and Michael Messner. 2017. "'From Fizzle to Sizzle!': Televised Sports News and the Production of Gender-Bland Sexism." *Gender and Society* 31, no. 5: 573–96.

Myskow, Wyatt, and Piper Hansen. 2020. "Incoming Cronkite Dean Has Alleged History of Racist, Homophobic Comments toward Students." *State Press*. https://www.statepress.com/article/2020/06/spcommunity-incoming-cronkite-dean-has-alleged-history-of-racist-homophobic-comments-toward-students.

Newell, Sean. 2016. "Clay Travis: The Real Victim of Online Harassment." *Vox*. https://www.vice.com/en_us/article/kbd5ny/clay-travis-the-real-victim-of-online-harassment.

Nguyen, Terry. 2020. "Natalie Portman's Oscars Cape Honors Snubbed Women Directors." *Vox*. https://www.vox.com/the-goods/2020/2/9/21130751/natalie-portman-oscars-cape-women-directors-the-academy.

Olson, Lisa. 1990. "A Lesson from 'The Chick.'" *Boston Herald*, 74.

———. 2017. "The #Metoo Movement Comes to Sports, a Reckoning Long Overdue." *Athletic*. https://theathletic.com/192516/2017/12/21/the-metoo-movement-comes-to-sports-a-reckoning-long-overdue/.

Papper, Bob. 2008. "Record Numbers for Women and Minorities." http://bobpapper.com/clients/.

Perez, Juan, and Bianca Quilantan. 2020. "How the New Devos Rules on Sexual Assault Will Shock Schools—and Students." *Politico.* https://www.politico.com/news/2020/03/06/betsy-devos-school-sexual-assault-rules-122401.

Ponder, Sam. 2013. "Examining Truth and Twitter." https://calvinistview.wordpress.com/2013/11/20/examining-truth-and-twitter/.

Ponder, Sam (@sam_ponder). 2014. "Blogs/websites that constantly disrespect women & objectify their bodies, then take a strong stand on the Ray Rice issue really confuse me." Tweet. https://twitter.com/sam_ponder/status/492482810590949377.

Portnoy, David. 2014. "Some Absolute Idiot Is Saying Sam Ponder's Twitter Feed Proves Her Point That Guys Who Objectify Women Don't Have the Right to Complain about Beating Women or Something." *Barstool Sports.* https://www.barstoolsports.com/boston/some-absolute-idiot-is-saying-sam-ponders-twitter-feed-proves-her-point-that-guys-who-objectify-women-dont-have-the-right-to-complain-about-beating-women-or-something/.

Raffel, William E. 2008. "Going Too Far: Language Limitations of Sports Talk Radio." *Journal of Radio and Audio Media* 15, no. 2: 197–208.

Rayno, Amelia. 2015. "Star Tribune's Amelia Rayno Adds Her Own Story to Teague Scandal." *Star Tribune.* http://www.startribune.com/star-tribune-s-rayno-adds-own-story-to-teague-scandal/321199871/.

"Richard Lapchick Study: 2014 Associated Press Sports Editors Racial and Gender Report Card." 2015. http://www.sportsbusinessnews.com/node/28342.

Rottenberg, Catherine. 2018. *The Rise of Neoliberal Feminism.* New York: Oxford University Press.

Ryan, Shannon. 2016. "Start Taking Female Sports Fans—and Their Impact—Seriously." *Chicago Tribune.* https://www.chicagotribune.com/sports/ct-sports-women-ryan-spt-1204-20161203-column.html.

Sainato, Michael. 2019. "'I Live on the Street Now': How Americans Fall into Medical Bankruptcy." *Guardian.* https://www.theguardian.com/us-news/2019/nov/14/health-insurance-medical-bankruptcy-debt.

Saks, Jeremy, and Molly Yanity. 2016. "The Not-So-Neutral Zone? ESPN, Agenda Setting, and the National Hockey League." *Journal of Sports Media* 11, no. 1: 81–100.

Schell, Lea Ann, and Stephanie Rodriguez. 2000. "Our Sporting Sisters: How Male Hegemony Stratifies Women in Sport." *Women in Sport and Physical Activity Journal* 9: 15–35.

Seltzer, Rick. 2018. "Missouri 3 Years Later: Lessons Learned, Protests Still Resonate." *Inside Higher Ed.* https://www.insidehighered.com/news/2018/09/12/administrators-students-and-activists-take-stock-three-years-after-2015-missouri.

Sheffer, Mary Lou, and Brad Schultz. 2007. "Double Standard: Why Women Have Trouble Getting Jobs in Local Television Sports." *Journal of Sports Media* 2, no. 1: 77–101.

Snyder, Marjorie A. 1993. "The New Competition: Sports Careers for Women." In *Women in Sports: Issues and Controversies*, edited by G. L. Cohen. Thousand Oaks CA: Sage.

Spain, Sarah. 2015. "I'm Mad as Hell & I'm Not Going to Take This Anymore." *Sarah Spain* (blog). http://sarahspain.com/im-mad-as-hell-im-not-going-to-take-this-anymore/.

Spain, Sarah (@SarahSpain). 2016. "So the shirt I wore literally a dozen years ago makes me deserving of hate. You guys prove my point over and over. #trash." Tweet. https://twitter.com/SarahSpain/status/725484212137107456.

Spanberg, Erik. 2018. "On the Air, On the Rise." *Sports Business Journal*. https://www.sportsbusinessdaily.com/Journal/Issues/2018/02/19/Media/NBA-women.aspx.

SportsMockery (@sportsmockery). 2016. "Must be the public's fault her top is falling off, she obviously didn't mean for you to see those." Tweet. https://twitter.com/sportsmockery/status/725432294303920128.

Strauss, Ben. 2018. "ESPN President Wants Less Politics at Network: 'It Is Not Our Jobs.'" *Washington Post*. https://www.washingtonpost.com/sports/espn-president-wants-less-politics-at-network-it-is-not-our-jobs-to-cover-politics/2018/08/17/6d54c706-a252-11e8-8e87-c869fe70a721_story.html.

Taylor, Maria (@MariaTaylor). 2020a. "Because I PLAYED basketball . . . I COVER the league. And I DESERVE everything I've worked hard for." Tweet. https://twitter.com/MariaTaylor/status/1307399244333146112.

———. 2020b. "Well Danny Dearest if you would like to continue making sexist comments about me . . . please bring your misogyny with you to the NBA Countdown double header I'll be hosting tomorrow night. Hey ladies remember you can wear whatever you feel confident in! @670TheScore @DannyMac670." Tweet. https://twitter.com/MariaTaylor/status/1305719693207121921.

———. 2020c. "Wow it's been a long week. But if everyone would now like to take away my voter privileges because of a CLEAR mistake. Please feel free." Tweet. https://twitter.com/MariaTaylor/status/1307398989994754050.

Teitell, Beth. 2017. "For at Least a Decade, Women Broadcasters Have Been Pushed to Look Sexier On-Air." *Boston Globe*. https://www.bostonglobe.com/metro/2017/08/14/why-newswomen-look-like-they-going-cocktail-party/AQq0w7piieQagmHCeFQ8IO/story.html.

"10 All-Star Female Sports Reporters." 2013. *Hollywood Reporter*. https://www.hollywoodreporter.com/gallery/10-all-star-female-sports-605094.

Travis, Clay. 2015a. "Is the Entire Mizzou Protest Based on Lies?" *Outkick the Coverage*. https://www.outkickthecoverage.com/is-the-entire-mizzou-protest-based-on-lies-111115/.

———. 2015b. "My Mom Reads Mean Tweets." *Outkick the Coverage*. https://www.outkickthecoverage.com/my-mom-reads-mean-tweets-051215/.

Travis, Clay (@ClayTravis). 2016a. "Here's my mom, a Southern grandma, reading a few of the mean Tweets sent to me. Her accent makes these great." Tweet. https://twitter.com/ClayTravis/status/724991927318241281.

——. 2016b. "I get murder threats on here regularly. People even threaten to kill my kids. That's Twitter." Tweet. https://twitter.com/ClayTravis/status /725007244757196801.

——. 2016c. "I'm confident that my mentions are tougher than 99.9% of all people, male or female, receive on Twitter." Tweet. https://twitter.com/ClayTravis /status/724989968066572289.

Trujillo, Nick. 1991. "Hegemonic Masculinity on the Mound: Media Representations of Nolan Ryan and American Sports Culture." *Critical Studies in Mass Communication* 8: 290–308.

Trump, Donald (@realDonaldTrump). 2017. "ESPN is paying a really big price for its politics (and bad programming). People are dumping it in RECORD numbers. Apologize for untruth!" Tweet. https://twitter.com/realDonaldTrump /status/908651641943003136.

Tuchman, Gaye. 1979. "Women's Depiction by the Mass Media." *Journal of Women in Culture and Society* 4, no. 3: 528–42.

Vinciguerra, Thomas. 2016. "The Long, Sordid History of Horribly Dressed Male Sportscasters." *Esquire*. http://www.esquire.com/style/a43272/history-of -sportscasters-bad-style/.

Wagner, Laura. 2018. "Sociopathic Barstool Founder David Portnoy Giddy about 'Suffocating' ESPN Host Sam Ponder in 'Online War.'" *Deadspin*. https://deadspin .com/sociopathic-barstool-founder-dave-portnoy-giddy-about-1829033370.

Watson, Graham (@SAEN_Graham). 2015a. "I have covered male sporting events all over the world and it took coming to Indianapolis to face my first gender discrimination." Tweet. https://twitter.com/SAEN_Graham/status/650785312851914752.

——. 2015b. "This guy was an usher and apparently not aware that women cover sports. I about lost it. @Colts @Jaguars." Tweet. https://twitter.com/SAEN _Graham/status/650784542924537856.

"Westwood One/CBS Radio Sports Announces Lesley Visser to Join NFL Monday Night Football Broadcast Team." 2001. *Business Wire*. https://web.archive.org /web/20071227100735/http://findarticles.com/p/articles/mi_m0EIN/is_2001 _June_26/ai_75894031.

Whitlock, Jason. 2020. "Maria Taylor Can Continue as 'The Unicorn' If She Avoids Nailing Herself to the Same Cross as Michelle Beadle and Jemele Hill." *Outkick*. https://www.outkick.com/maria-taylor-doug-gottlieb-michelle-beadle -and-jemele-hill/.

Whitlock, Jason (@WhitlockJason). 2016a. "Twitter isn't remotely a safe space. Everyone who states an opinion from an elevated platform gets mean tweets. #womenandmenblackandwhite." Tweet. https://twitter.com/WhitlockJason/status /724994113649532928.

——. 2016b. "Waging a campaign against Twitter eggs is the work of sheep. It's a public-relations campaign for Social Justice Warriors." Tweet. https://twitter .com/WhitlockJason/status/725097133209169920.

Index

To order or obtain more information on these or other
University of Nebraska Press titles, visit nebraskapress.unl.edu.

CPSIA information can be obtained
at www.ICGtesting.com
Printed in the USA
LVHW031126020721
691689LV00004B/370